DICTIONARY OF SOCIAL WORK A-Z

Mark Richard

In the world of social work, which is so rich in terms, practices, and concepts, a reliable reference book is important. This book was created to fill that gap.

Social work, a dynamic and multifaceted field, touches on numerous aspects of human life. From supporting families in crisis situations to promoting social participation to the rehabilitation and integration of people with special needs - social work is an essential part of our society.

This dictionary provides a comprehensive overview of the key terms, concepts, and practices of social work. From the basic principles to the current developments and challenges, it covers a wide range that appeals to both students and professionals.

Our goal is to create a valuable tool that not only serves to explain terms, but also helps to develop a deeper understanding of the complexity and importance of social work.

We hope that this book is not only a reference work, but also a source of inspiration for all those working in this important field.

Table of contents

Addiction Counseling

Addiction counseling is an important area of social work that deals with the prevention, counseling, and support of people with addiction problems. Addiction can take various forms, e.g. alcohol and drug addiction, gambling addiction, eating disorders, etc. The aim of addiction counselling is to help those affected overcome their addiction and lead an addiction-free life.

Advice and information:
- Addiction counseling includes counseling sessions in which sufferers and their relatives receive information about addiction, its effects, and treatment options. Education plays a crucial role in raising awareness of the issue of addiction.

Diagnosis and Assessment:
- Addiction counselors perform a comprehensive diagnosis and evaluation to understand the severity of the addiction problem. This allows for the development of an individualized treatment plan.

Therapeutic interventions:
- Addiction counseling includes various therapeutic interventions, including cognitive behavioral therapy, talk therapy, motivational support, and other approaches to support behavior change.

Individual and group counselling:
- Both individual counseling and group counseling are common forms of addiction counseling. One-on-one counseling allows for one-on-one care, while group counseling encourages the sharing of experiences and support among like-minded people.

Relapse prevention:

- Addiction counseling involves the development of strategies for relapse prevention. This includes identifying risk situations, developing coping strategies, and promoting life skills.

Counselling for relatives:

- Addiction counselling often involves relatives as well. The support of family and friends is important to strengthen the environment of the affected person and prevent relapses.

Mediation in therapy and withdrawal:

- If necessary, referral is made to further treatment measures such as inpatient or outpatient therapy programs and withdrawal treatments.

Prevention and education:

- Addiction counseling also includes preventive measures to educate people about the risks of addiction and raise awareness about addiction prevention.

Social Work and Support Services:

- Social workers in addiction counseling can provide support services to help manage social challenges that may arise from addiction. This may include dealing with legal issues, homelessness, or workplace issues.

Cooperation with other institutions:

- Addiction counsellors often work closely with other organisations, including hospitals, clinics, support groups, employment services, and legal services, to provide comprehensive support.

Cultural Sensitivity:

- Addiction counseling must be culturally sensitive and take into account the diverse needs of different population groups.

Ethics and confidentiality:

- Ethics and confidentiality are of paramount importance in addiction counseling. Advisors must adhere to ethical standards and ensure that the privacy of those affected is protected.

Addiction counseling plays a crucial role in helping people on the road to recovery and preventing relapse. Crucial to the success of addiction counseling is an integrative approach that takes individual needs into account.

Aid

Assistive devices are technical or technological instruments, apparatus or devices that help people with physical or mental disabilities to maintain their independence, improve their quality of life and participate in social life. Assistive devices can be used in various areas of life.

Mobility aids:
- Wheelchairs, walkers, walkers, crutches, and electric mobility aids are examples of assistive devices that support the mobility of people with physical limitations.

Aids for coping with everyday life:
- Gripping aids, dressing aids, cutlery with ergonomic handles, non-slip mats and other aids make everyday activities easier for people with limited motor skills.

Tools for communication:
- Communication aids, such as voice computers, videophones or special apps for smartphones, can support people with speech or communication disorders.

Hearing aids:

- Hearing aids, cochlear implants and other hearing aids improve the hearing ability of people with hearing impairments.

Visual aids:

- Magnifiers, screen readers, Braille displays and other visual aids support people with visual impairments.

Assistive devices in the living area:

- Adaptations in the living space, such as grab bars, stair lifts, shower seats or special beds, can help people stay longer in their familiar surroundings.

Electronic aids:

- Smart home technologies, sensors and automated systems can help people manage their everyday lives more autonomously. This can include, for example, the control of lighting, heating or safety devices.

Orthopaedic aids:

- Orthopaedic shoes, insoles, bandages and orthoses are examples of aids that are used to support or correct bodily functions.

Aids for care:

- Care beds, care aids, lifts and other specialized equipment make it easier to care for people with reduced mobility or other health problems.

Financing of aids:

- In many countries, the cost of certain aids is covered by health insurance, long-term care insurance, or other government agencies. The exact regulations vary depending on the country and the type of aid.

Customization:

- Assistive devices should be individually adapted to the needs and abilities of the users. Professional advice and adjustment by professionals, such as occupational therapists or orthopaedic technicians, is often necessary.

Assistive devices play a crucial role in enabling people with disabilities to be more independent, secure and participate in society. However, the selection and adaptation of assistive devices should always be tailored to the individual needs and abilities of the user.

Anamnesis

The medical history is the systematic collection of information about a patient's history and current condition by a healthcare professional. It is an essential part of the diagnostic process and is used to gather relevant information to allow an accurate assessment of the state of health.

Anamnesis:
- The medical history involves systematically questioning the patient about various aspects of their health history, including symptoms, pre-existing conditions, medication use, family history, lifestyle, psychosocial factors, and other relevant information.

Objectives of the anamnesis:

Understanding symptoms: Identifying the nature and duration of current complaints or symptoms to identify possible causes.

Existing medical conditions: Identification of previously diagnosed medical conditions or chronic health problems.

Risk factors: Identify risk factors that could affect health, such as genetic predispositions, lifestyle factors, or occupational exposures.

Medication history: Recording of the medication currently being taken as well as any allergies or intolerances.

Carrying out the anamnesis:

- The medical history is usually in the form of a structured conversation between the patient and the healthcare provider, whether it is a doctor, nurse practitioner, or therapist.
- Standardized questionnaires, physical examinations, and laboratory tests can be included to gather additional information.

Timeline:

- The anamnesis spans various points in time, starting with the patient's medical history and ending with the patient's current symptoms. The time course can help to understand changes in health status.

Documentation:

- All information collected during the anamnesis is carefully documented. This documentation serves as the basis for diagnosis, treatment planning, and monitoring of the patient over time.

Through a comprehensive medical history, healthcare providers can provide the best possible care by understanding and taking into account the patient's individual needs and circumstances.

Assistance for young adults

Assistance for young adults refers to support services and measures offered to young people in the transition from youth welfare to self-employment and adult life. This transition is often particularly challenging, as young people need to develop their independence and prepare for a self-reliant life during this phase.

Youth welfare after the 18th birthday:
- In many countries, regular youth welfare ends when the child reaches the age of majority. Assistance for young adults is intended to ensure that support is still available when necessary.

Extension of youth welfare:
- In many countries, there are regulations for the extension of youth welfare beyond the age of 18. This enables continuous support when needed, for example in finding housing, training or professional integration.

Housing and residential care:
- A key aspect of support for young adults is the provision of housing. This can include assistance in finding your own apartment or the possibility of assisted living.

Training and career development:
- Assistance for young adults often includes measures to promote training and professional integration. This may include assistance in finding apprenticeships or jobs, job application training, and financial support for education costs.

Financial support:
- Young adults may receive financial support to meet their basic needs. This may include rent subsidies, alimony, or financial assistance for living expenses.

Socio-pedagogical support:

- Socio-pedagogical support plays an important role in helping young adults. This can include counselling, support in life planning, coping with everyday problems and promoting social skills.

Preventive health care and psychosocial support:

- Promoting physical and mental health is crucial. Assistance may include preventive health services, psychosocial support, and access to medical care.

Networking and integration in communities:

- Support for young adults often includes networking and community integration activities. This may include participation in recreational activities, sports or cultural events.

Family-related support:

- In some cases, family-related support is also offered if contact with the family continues to be important and conducive to the development of the young adult.

Legal advice:

- Legal advice can be part of the support, especially when it comes to issues such as tenancy law, employment law or other legal matters.

The assistance for young adults is intended to help them make the transition to self-employment. The assistance should be individually tailored, take into account the needs and goals of the young person and accompany him or her on the way to an independent life.

Assistance services

Assistance services refer to supportive measures that help people with different needs to maintain their independence, improve their quality of life and participate fully in social life. Assistance services can be required in different areas of life and take different forms. Some examples:

Personal Assistance:
- Assist with personal activities of daily living, such as dressing, washing, eating, and mobility. This is especially relevant for people with physical impairments.

Accompanying assistance:
- Accompaniment and support for activities outside the home, such as shopping, doctor's visits, social events or leisure activities.

Technical Assistance:
- Use of technological tools to promote self-reliance. This may include, for example, the use of wheelchairs, walking aids, hearing aids, or other technical devices.

Work Assistance:
- Workplace support to support people with disabilities or special needs in their professional activities. This may include workplace adaptation, special training or individual support.

Nursing Assistance:
- Nursing support that goes beyond activities of daily living, such as administering medication, wound care, or other nursing measures.

Communicative Assistance:

- Assistance for people with communication impairments, be it through communication support, sign language or the use of communication aids.

Social Assistance:

- Support in maintaining social contacts and participating in social activities. This can be especially important for people who have difficulty with social interaction due to limitations.

Financial Assistance:

- Advice and assistance in dealing with financial matters, including applying for financial benefits or assisting with budget planning.

Advisory Assistance:

- Counselling services to help people overcome challenges, whether related to personal concerns, mental health, education or professional development.

Family Assistance:

- Supporting family members who take on the care and support of people with special needs. This may include training, psychosocial support and respite services.

Assistance services are individually tailored to the needs of the person concerned and may be required temporarily or permanently. They help people to lead a self-determined life despite special challenges.

Basic income support

Basic income support is a form of social support that has been introduced in some countries to ensure a minimum financial subsistence level for certain groups of people.

Aim of basic income support:
- The main goal of basic income support is to ensure a living income for people who cannot earn a living from their own resources. This usually applies to people of retirement age or people with a permanent disability.

Circle:
- The entitlement to basic income support is often aimed at older people who do not receive an adequate pension, as well as at people who are permanently reduced in earning capacity and are therefore unable to earn a living from their own gainful employment.

Types of basic income support:
- Basic income support can take various forms, such as basic security in old age and in the event of reduced earning capacity. The exact designation and design may vary from country to country.

Needs assessment:
- Similar to social assistance, a needs assessment is also carried out in the case of basic income support in order to determine the individual need for financial support. The applicant's income and assets are taken into account.

Principle of subordination:
- Basic income support often follows the principle of subordination, which means that benefits are only granted when all other possible options for help and support, such as one's own pension, have been exhausted.

Income and asset imputation:

- The applicant's income and assets are taken into account when calculating the basic income. There are allowances, and certain income or assets are not taken into account.

Application Process:

- In order to receive basic security, an application must usually be submitted to the responsible social welfare office. Here, too, it is necessary to disclose one's personal and financial circumstances.

Amount of benefits:

- The amount of basic income support is based on the applicant's needs and is calculated on the basis of fixed standard rates as well as individual needs.

Social status:

- The social status and the requirements for the granting of basic income may vary from country to country. There are specific laws and regulations that regulate basic security.

Basic income support plays an important role in protecting older people and people with permanent disability from poverty and enabling them to lead a dignified life.

Benefits for participation in working life

Benefits for participation in working life are measures and aids that are intended to enable people with health restrictions to participate fully or partially in working life. These benefits are intended to ensure that people can work despite health restrictions.

Vocational rehabilitation:

- Vocational rehabilitation includes measures aimed at integrating or reintegrating people with health impairments into the labour market. This may include retraining, further training or special qualification measures.

Workplace adaptations:

- Benefits for participation in working life may include adaptation of the workplace. This includes structural changes, the provision of technical aids or the adjustment of working hours to meet individual needs.

Work aids and equipment:

- People with health restrictions may need special work equipment or equipment in order to be able to carry out their professional tasks successfully. These include, for example, ergonomic office chairs, screen readers or other technical aids.

Support from integration services:

- In some countries, there are specialist integration services that support people with disabilities and employers in successfully integrating into the workplace. These services offer advice, mediation and support.

Personal budgets:

- In some systems, people with disabilities have the option of receiving a personal budget. With this budget, they can finance individually tailored support services that promote their participation in working life.

Integration grants for employers:

- In order to make it easier for employers to recruit people with disabilities, integration grants may be granted. These financial incentives are intended to motivate companies to hire people with health impairments.

Work Assistance:

- Work assistants are individual accompaniments at the workplace that support people with disabilities. This can include training, guidance on special tasks or support in everyday work.

Participation Counselling:

- Participation counselling offers individual advice and support to promote participation in working life. This may include the identification of appropriate measures and support services.

Rehabilitation allowance and transitional allowance:

- In some countries, people who are no longer able to work due to health reasons can receive rehabilitation or transitional allowances. This serves to provide financial security during vocational rehabilitation.

Participation in working life for people with mental illnesses:

- Special measures and programmes are often needed to support people with mental illness in their participation in working life. This may include therapeutic support, flexible time management, and other adjustments.

Benefits for participation in working life aim to create optimal conditions for people with health impairments to be professionally active and to contribute their individual skills to the workplace.

Career Information Centre

The Career Information Centre is an institution that provides information and advice on various job-related topics. These centres are contact points for people who are looking for guidance and information about professions, training, courses of study and career opportunities.

Guidance:

- They provide resources and support for individuals who want to better understand their professional interests and skills. This may include tests, questionnaires, or face-to-face counseling.

Training and study counselling:

- Information on various training and study opportunities is provided. The Career Information Centre can provide information on the prerequisites, content and perspectives of various training courses and degree programmes.

Job profiles and labour market information:

- BIZs provide comprehensive information on various job profiles, including descriptions of jobs, qualifications, and career prospects. They also provide information about the current job market and trends in specific industries.

Application and career planning:

- Advice on application processes, CV preparation and interviews are often part of the services of a Career Information Centre. They can also support long-term career planning and development.

Opportunities:

- Information on further education and training opportunities will be provided. This can include both formal educational institutions and informal continuing education programmes.

Work and international experience:

- Career Information Centres can also provide information on job opportunities abroad, international exchange programs, and internships to broaden the horizons of work experience.

Digital Resources:

- Many Career Information Centres also offer digital resources, including online platforms, comprehensive websites, and interactive tools to facilitate access to information.

Events and workshops:
- Career Information Centres often organize events, seminars, and workshops on various job-related topics. These can include presentations by professionals, job fairs, or hands-on training.

Career information centres are usually free or low-cost and are designed to help people plan and develop their careers. They are particularly relevant for pupils, students, young professionals and people who are planning a career change.

Case Management

Case management is a process-oriented, person-centered approach that aims to provide comprehensive support to people and coordinate their needs in different areas of life. It is used in various contexts, including healthcare, social work, rehabilitation and other service sectors.

Person-centered approach:
- The focus of case management is on the individual. It's about understanding and aligning with the needs, goals, and preferences of the person concerned.

Holistic view:
- Case management takes into account the different areas of a person's life, including health, education, housing, social

integration, and more. The goal is to provide comprehensive support.

Coordination of services:

- One of the main tasks of case management is to coordinate services. This means ensuring that different service providers and professionals work together effectively to meet the needs of the data subject.

Needs assessment and planning:

- Case managers conduct a comprehensive assessment of needs and resources. Based on this, an individual support plan is created, which includes the steps to achieve the set goals.

Communication and Collaboration:

- Case management requires effective communication and collaboration between all parties involved, including the affected person, their family, medical professionals, social workers, therapists, and other service providers.

Monitoring and evaluation:

- The progress of case management is continuously monitored and evaluated to ensure that the set goals are met and to make adjustments as needs change.

Empowerment and self-determination:

- Case management aims to promote the self-determination and empowerment of the person concerned. This means involving them in the decision-making process and strengthening their autonomy.

Time limit:

- Case management is often temporary, and support is usually adjusted or terminated once the goals set have been achieved and the person concerned is able to move forward independently.

Flexibility and adaptability:

- Because people's needs are diverse and can change over time, case management requires some flexibility and adaptability.

Ethics and confidentiality:
- Case managers operate according to ethical standards and respect the confidentiality of the information collected during the process.

Case management is used in various fields, such as healthcare, social work, rehabilitation, elderly care, and other social services. It offers a structured approach to support people in complex life situations and improve their quality of life.

Client-centricity

Client-centeredness is a conceptual approach that is applied in various fields, especially in the social, health and therapeutic contexts. It emphasizes the active involvement and orientation towards the needs, wishes and perspectives of the clients.

Individual needs and wishes:
- Client-centricity focuses on the individual needs, wishes and goals of the client. Every person is considered unique, and the services are adapted accordingly.

Partnership-based cooperation:
- Client-centricity is based on a partnership between the service providers and the clients. It is emphasized that clients should be active partners in decision-making processes.

Self-determination and autonomy:
- A central principle of client-centeredness is the promotion of self-determination and autonomy. Clients should be able to make decisions about their own lives.

Empowerment:
- Empowerment is an important aspect of client centricity. The approach aims to empower clients to use their own resources and play an active role in their own well-being.

Respect for diversity:
- Client-centeredness embraces cultural diversity and respects different backgrounds, values, and beliefs. The approach is designed to recognise the individuality and diversity of the clients.

Active listener:
- Service providers, therapists or social workers take an active listening role. Clients' concerns and needs are taken seriously and listened to attentively.

Common objectives:
- Goals are set together with the clients. The services are designed to support and promote the individual goals of the clients.

Flexibility and customization:
- Client-centricity requires flexibility and the ability to tailor services according to clients' changing needs and progress.

Holistic approach:
- Client-centeredness takes a holistic view of the person and integrates physical, emotional, social and cultural aspects into the support processes.

Feedback and evaluation:
- Regular feedback from clients is an integral part of client centricity. Evaluations help to check the effectiveness of the services and to make adjustments if necessary.

Continuity of care:

- Client-centricity strives for continuous care to ensure long-term and sustainable support. Continuity fosters trust and a stronger relationship.

Customer centricity represents a paradigm shift that shifts the focus from the institution or service provider to the individual needs and perspectives of the customer.

Client's perspective

The customer perspective refers to the point of view, experiences, needs and opinions of the people who use services or support, whether in social, health, professional or other contexts. Consideration of the client's perspective is an essential aspect in various fields, especially in social and therapeutic professions.

Empathy and respect:

- The client perspective emphasizes the importance of empathy and respect for the individual experiences and needs of the clients. This includes acknowledging the uniqueness of each person.

Participation and co-determination:

- A client-centered perspective promotes the active participation of clients in decision-making processes, planning and goal formulation. The individual ideas and goals of the clients should be taken seriously.

Needs orientation:
- The client's perspective emphasizes understanding the individual needs of the clients and responding accordingly. This can mean customizing services and responding flexibly to changes in clients' needs.

Empowerment:
- The client's perspective includes the pursuit of empowerment, i.e. the strengthening of self-determination and personal responsibility of the clients. The aim is for them to be empowered to use their own resources and find solutions to their concerns.

Transparency and communication:
- Clear and open communication is crucial. Clients should be informed about their rights, the type of support offered and the possible consequences. Transparency fosters trust.

Cultural Sensitivity:
- The client's perspective takes into account cultural diversity and respects different backgrounds, values and beliefs. Cultural sensitivity is important in order to adequately understand and respond to the needs of different groups.

Feedback and evaluation:
- Clients' opinions are actively sought and integrated into the service process. Feedback mechanisms and evaluations help to improve the quality of services.

Self-determination and autonomy:
- The client's perspective promotes the self-determination and autonomy of the clients. This means supporting their skills and resources so that they can make decisions on their own.

Continuity of care:
- Continuity of care is important to ensure long-term and sustainable support. This builds trust and allows services to be continuously adapted to changing needs.

Protection of privacy:

- The protection of privacy and confidentiality is essential. The client perspective respects the privacy of the clients and ensures that information is kept confidential.

Taking the customer's perspective into account helps to better tailor services to individual needs, promote customer satisfaction, and improve positive outcomes.

Coaching

Coaching is an interactive, goal-oriented process in which a coach assists an individual or group in clarifying, developing, and achieving their personal or professional goals. Coaching can be used in a variety of contexts, including professional development, personal growth, leadership, teamwork, and more.

Goal orientation:

- Coaching focuses on clarifying and achieving clear goals. The coachee (the person being coached) defines the goals, and the coach supports them in identifying ways to achieve them.

Self-reflection:

- Coaching promotes self-reflection. The coachee is encouraged to reflect on their beliefs, values, skills, and behavioral patterns in order to gain a better understanding of themselves.

Confidentiality:

- Coaching is based on trust. The coach is committed to confidentiality in order to create a safe space for open conversations where the coachee can speak without worrying about judgment.

Questions and Feedback:

- The coach asks questions to stimulate the coachee's thinking and support them in finding solutions. Feedback is given constructively and encouragingly to encourage learning.

Empowerment:

- Coaching aims to empower the coachee. The focus is on increasing self-confidence, promoting personal responsibility and developing self-leadership skills.

Tailor-made approaches:

- Coaching approaches are individually tailored to the needs of the coachee. There are no hard and fast rules or predefined solutions; instead, strategies are developed that are suitable for the specific situation.

Holistic approach:

- Coaching can encompass various areas of life, including professional, personal, and social aspects. A holistic approach takes into account that these areas are interconnected.

Skill Development:

- Coaching helps to develop skills and competencies. This can include both professional and personal skills, from communication and time management to emotional intelligence and leadership skills.

Measurability and evaluation:

- Successes and progress in the coaching process are measurable and can be evaluated. This helps to keep the focus on goal achievement and adjust the coaching process when necessary.

Short- and long-term focus:
- Coaching can include both short-term and long-term goals. Individual sessions can focus on current challenges, while the entire process can help achieve long-term development goals.

Coaching can be provided by professional coaches who are specifically trained for this role or by internal coaches in companies and organizations. The success of coaching depends heavily on the cooperation between coach and coachee as well as on the coachee's openness to change and personal growth.

Collegial advice

Collegial counselling is a form of exchange and support among colleagues within an organisation. The aim is to support each other with professional challenges, problems or development issues and to work out solutions together.

Equivalence:
- In the collegial consultation, all participants are recognized as equal partners. Hierarchical differences are largely eliminated for the duration of the counselling situation.

Confidentiality:
- Similar to individual counselling, confidentiality is an important principle. Everything that is discussed in the

collegial consultation remains between the colleagues involved.

Voluntariness:

- Participation in peer counselling is usually voluntary. Colleagues decide for themselves whether they want to get involved in such a consulting situation.

Solution orientation:

- The focus of collegial counselling is on the joint search for solutions to professional challenges. It's about bringing in constructive ideas and perspectives to identify solutions.

Structured forms of conversation:

- Depending on your needs, collegial consultations can be structured. There are different models and methods that can be used to organize the counseling process.

Feedback Culture:

- The collegial advice promotes an open feedback culture. Colleagues give each other constructive feedback based on honesty, respect, and appreciation.

Case-relatedness:

- Collegial advice often refers to specific cases or situations that a colleague is confronted with. This enables practical and application-oriented advice.

Development Promotion:

- In addition to solving problems, collegial counselling also serves professional and personal development. Colleagues can learn from each other and develop their skills.

Reflection and self-clarification:

- Participants will have the opportunity to reflect on their thoughts and ideas. Collegial counselling promotes self-clarification and conscious engagement with professional challenges.

Diversity of perspectives:

- Through the participation of colleagues from different fields or with different experiences, collegial counseling brings a variety of perspectives to the consulting process.

Flexibility in terms of time:

- Collegial counselling can take place in formal meetings or informal conversations. The flexibility in terms of time allows participants to choose the forms that are suitable for them.

Collegial counselling is a valuable addition to formal support structures in organisations. It promotes the exchange of knowledge, strengthens team spirit and contributes to the achievement of individual and common professional goals.

Communication

Communication is a central element in various social, professional and personal contexts. It involves the exchange of information, ideas, thoughts, and feelings between individuals or groups.

Verbal communication:

- Verbal communication refers to the use of words, whether spoken or written. This includes verbal conversations, phone calls, text messages, written reports, and other forms of verbal interaction.

Non-verbal communication:

- Non-verbal communication involves the transmission of information without the use of words. This can be done through body language, facial expressions, gestures, eye contact, posture, and other nonverbal cues.

Interpersonal communication:

- Interpersonal communication refers to the exchange of information between two or more people. Here, the quality of the relationship, emotional intelligence and the ability to listen play a decisive role.

Communication channels:

- Various communication channels are available, including face-to-face conversations, phone calls, written communications, emails, social media, and more. The choice of communication channel often depends on the nature of the information and the relationship.

Active listening:

- Active listening is a key component of effective communication. It involves being really present, understanding the interlocutor's utterances and responding to them appropriately.

Communication styles:

- People have different communication styles that are influenced by their personality, cultural background, and other factors. An understanding of different communication styles contributes to successful interaction.

Feedback:

- Feedback is an essential part of communication. It makes it possible to check the understanding and helps to clarify misunderstandings. Constructive feedback fosters a positive culture of communication.

Communication in conflict situations:

- In conflict situations, clear and respectful communication is particularly important. The ability to approach and resolve conflicts constructively helps strengthen relationships.

Communication technologies:

- Advances in technology have enabled new forms of communication, from video conferencing to social media. The effective use of communication technology requires an understanding of its advantages and disadvantages.

Cultural Sensitivity:
- Cultural sensitivity is important to avoid misunderstandings due to cultural differences. This includes taking into account cultural norms, values, and communication styles.

Communication in a professional context:
- In a professional environment, clear and concise communication is crucial. Sharing clear instructions, writing reports, giving presentations, and collaborating as a team require effective communication skills.

Self-reflection:
- Self-reflection on one's own communication is important in order to recognize one's own strengths and weaknesses and to continuously improve communication skills.

Effective communication is crucial for understanding, collaboration, and relationship building. It is a dynamic process that requires constant adaptation and maintenance.

Communication training

Communication training is targeted training to improve communication skills and techniques. This can be done in different contexts, be it professional, social or personal.

Active listening:
- The training often focuses on the development of active listening, which means not only listening to the words of

the interlocutor, but also understanding their emotions and perspectives.

Clarity and precision:

- One focus is on developing the ability to convey clear and concise messages. This includes choosing appropriate words, avoiding misunderstandings, and clarity in communication.

Body language and non-verbal communication:

- Communication training often includes raising awareness of body language and nonverbal signals. Participants will learn how their posture, facial expressions and gestures can influence their communication.

Constructive feedback:

- The ability to give and receive constructive feedback is an important part of training. This fosters an open communication culture and supports personal and professional development.

Conflict:

- Communication training can teach strategies for effective conflict management. This includes techniques for de-escalation, conflict resolution, and dealing with differing opinions.

Self-reflection:

- Participants are encouraged to reflect on themselves and recognize their own communication patterns. This allows for more conscious and improved communication.

Emotional Intelligence:

- Communication training can promote the development of emotional intelligence, which includes the ability to recognize, understand, and respond appropriately to emotions.

Team Communication:

- In a professional context, the training can be aimed at improving team communication. This includes fostering clear team goals, effective meetings, and collaborative collaboration.

Communication technologies:

- Since technology plays an important role in communication, training can include the effective use of email, video conferencing, and other digital communication tools.

Self-presentation and public speaking:

- Communication training can improve skills in the area of self-presentation and public speaking. This is especially relevant for professional contexts where presentations and meetings take place.

Communication in different contexts:

- Depending on your needs, the training can cover specific aspects of communication in different contexts, whether in sales, customer service, leadership or interpersonal relationships.

The goal of communication training is to enable participants to communicate more effectively, minimize misunderstandings, manage conflicts, and build positive relationships.

Conflict Resolution Techniques

Conflicts are inevitable in both professional and personal life. The ability to resolve conflicts constructively is crucial for healthy interpersonal dynamics.

Improve communication:
- Clear and open communication is crucial. Everyone should have the opportunity to share their perspective without interruptions. Active listening is essential to fully understand what the other person is saying.

Looking for a win-win solution:
- Instead of looking for a winner and a loser, aim for solutions where all parties can win. This requires creativity and flexibility in finding common interests.

Clarity about needs and interests:
- Conflicts often arise from different needs and interests. A clear identification of these interests can lay the foundation for conflict resolution.

Developing empathy:
- Empathy, empathizing with each other's feelings and perspectives, is crucial. It helps to promote understanding and create an emotionally positive atmosphere.

De-escalation techniques:
- De-escalation techniques help reduce tension. These include controlling one's temperament, slowing down the pace of the conversation, and avoiding aggressive gestures.

Neutral mediation:
- A neutral mediator can help resolve conflicts, especially if the parties involved have difficulty talking to each other directly. This person should be impartial and take into account everyone's interests.

Make clear agreements:
- At the end of a conflict resolution, clear agreements should be reached. These agreements should be specific, realistic and measurable in order to increase the likelihood of compliance.

Showing a willingness to compromise:
- Willingness to compromise is important in order to find a solution that all parties can live with. It requires a

willingness to renounce some demands in order to find common ground.

Give time to cool down:

- Sometimes it's helpful to take a break to cool tempers. This can give stakeholders a chance to gather their thoughts and think more rationally about the situation.

Conflict prevention:

- Preventive measures can help prevent conflicts in advance. This can include conflict resolution training, clear communication guidelines, and a positive organizational culture.

Analysis of the underlying causes:

- Analyzing the underlying causes of a conflict can help identify recurring problems and find long-term solutions.

Use feedback:

- Gathering feedback after conflict resolution can help improve the process and strengthen relationships.

The application of these techniques requires practice and constant reflection. The ability to resolve conflicts is a valuable skill that not only strengthens personal relationships, but also promotes the efficiency and productivity of teams and organizations.

Constructivism

Constructivism is a pedagogical and philosophical theory that deals with how people construct knowledge and create meaning from their experiences. This perspective emphasizes that learning is an active process in which individuals actively build knowledge by linking new information to their existing knowledge and experiences.

Active learning process:
- In constructivism, learning is seen as an active process in which individuals actively process, interpret, and integrate information into their own mental structures.

Self-reliant learning:
- The responsibility for the learning process lies with the learner himself. This means that learners are actively searching for meaning, rather than simply passively absorbing information.

Existing knowledge:
- Constructivism emphasizes the importance of the individual's existing knowledge and experience. New knowledge is built on the basis of what the person already knows and understands.

Social Learning:
- The social aspect of learning is of great importance to constructivism. Learning is considered a social process in which interactions with other people help to construct knowledge.

Collaborative Learning:
- Collaborative learning, in which individuals work together on tasks and share their knowledge, is considered an effective way to create meaning together.

Application-oriented learning:
- The focus is on applying knowledge in real-life situations. Learners should be able to apply their knowledge to new contexts and problems.

Contextualized Learning:
- Learning is considered contextualized in constructivism. The context in which learning takes place significantly influences the construction of knowledge.

Learners as problem solvers:
- Learners are seen as active problem solvers. The focus is on teaching them the skills to understand, analyze and develop solutions to complex problems.

Feedback and reflection:
- Feedback is seen as an important part of the learning process. Through regular feedback, learners can review and improve their own thinking and strategies.

Diversity of perspectives:
- Constructivism acknowledges that different people have different perspectives and interpretations. Diversity is seen as an enrichment for the learning process.

Lifelong learning:
- Constructivism promotes the idea of lifelong learning. Learning is seen as an ongoing process that goes beyond formal educational institutions.

Constructivism has had a significant impact on pedagogical approaches and has led to a change in teaching methods that are more focused on creating learning environments that correspond to the constructive processes of learners. This theory influences not only the field of education, but also other fields such as psychology, sociology, and communication.

Consultation

Counseling is a process in which a qualified individual or group of professionals provides information, support, and guidance to help people overcome challenges, solve problems, or achieve goals. Counseling can be offered in a variety of contexts, including personal, professional, social, or health settings.

Aim of the consultation:
- The main goal of counseling is to help people understand their problems, bring about positive change, make decisions, and improve their quality of life.

Confidentiality:
- Advice is based on confidentiality. Counsellors are obliged to respect the privacy of their clients and not to disclose information without consent.

Empathy and acceptance:
- Counsellors should be empathetic and accept their clients. This means understanding and respecting clients' feelings and perspectives.

Counselling methods:
- There are different counseling methods and approaches, depending on the needs of the clients and the context of the counseling. These include cognitive behavioral therapy, talk therapy, solution-oriented counseling, and others.

Fields of Expertise:
- Counseling can be offered in many different areas, including psychological counseling, school counseling, marriage and family counseling, career counseling, addiction counseling, financial counseling, and more.

Preventive advice:
- In addition to providing support for existing problems, counselling can also be used preventively to prevent crises, strengthen resources and build resilience.

Crisis intervention:
- In acute crisis situations, counseling provides rapid support and intervention to ensure the safety and well-being of clients.

Counselling in a group context:

- Counselling can take place individually or in groups. Group counseling offers the opportunity to learn from the experiences of others and receive support in a community setting.

Cultural Sensitivity:

- Counsellors need to be culturally sensitive and take into account the diversity of their clientele. This includes the recognition of different cultural backgrounds, values and norms.

Counseling Ethics:

- Consultants follow a code of ethics designed to ensure their professionalism and integrity. This includes clear boundaries, the renunciation of personal value judgments, and a commitment to ongoing professional development.

Counselling plays an important role in supporting people in different life situations. It provides a safe space for reflection, personal development and the search for solutions to personal or professional challenges.

Cooperation

Cooperation refers to the cooperation of individuals, groups, or organizations to achieve common goals or accomplish tasks. Cooperation is an important aspect in various contexts, be it social, economic, scientific or political.

Common goals:
- Cooperation is often based on striving to achieve common goals. Individuals or groups work together to achieve results that are beneficial to all parties involved.

Communication:
- Effective communication is crucial for successful cooperation. Clear and open communication allows stakeholders to share information, clarify expectations, and avoid misunderstandings.

Sharing of resources:
- In cooperative relationships, resources are often shared. This may include material resources, knowledge, skills, or other aspects that contribute to the achievement of the common goals.

Trust:
- Trust is a fundamental element of cooperation. Stakeholders must be able to trust that their partners will fulfil their obligations and that cooperation will be based on mutual benefit.

Conflict resolution:
- Conflicts can arise in any collaboration. The ability to resolve conflicts constructively is crucial to maintain and develop collaboration.

Mutual assistance:
- In a collaborative environment, the participants support each other. This may include providing emotional support, helping to overcome challenges, or providing resources.

Flexibility:
- Cooperation often requires flexibility, as conditions and requirements can change over time. The ability to adapt and find solutions together is important.

Division of responsibilities:
- The clear division of responsibilities and roles helps ensure that each partner can contribute. This minimizes uncertainties and promotes efficiency.

Learning and Innovation:

- Cooperation offers the opportunity to learn from each other and develop innovative solutions. The exchange of ideas and perspectives fosters creativity and continuous improvement.

Shared decision-making:

- In collaborative efforts, it is important to involve all stakeholders in the decision-making process. Joint decisions promote commitment and identification with the goals.

Social Responsibility:

- In cooperative relationships, social responsibility is often emphasized. This may mean that partners not only pursue their own interests, but also have the good of the community in mind.

Long-term relationships:

- Cooperation is often aimed at building long-term relationships. This requires continuity, reliability and the willingness to tackle challenges together.

Cooperation plays an important role in various social, economic and cultural contexts. Not only does it enable the achievement of common goals, but it also helps to strengthen relationships and foster innovation and growth.

Coping

"Coping" refers to the coping strategies and mechanisms that people use to deal with stress, challenges, stressful situations, or changes in life. It is a multidimensional concept that encompasses emotional, cognitive, behavioral, and social aspects.

Coping:
- Coping involves various strategies that people use to deal with stress. These include emotional coping, problem-oriented coping, seeking social support, avoidance, positive reinterpretation, and more.

Emotional coping:
- Emotional coping refers to how people regulate their emotions in stressful situations. This can include expressing emotions, finding emotional support, or applying relaxation techniques.

Problem-oriented management:
- This is about actively working to solve the problem that is causing the stress. This can include planning, analysis of options for action and strategic approach.

Acceptance and Adaptation:
- Sometimes coping involves accepting immutable circumstances and adapting to new realities. This approach can help minimize the effects of stress and promote mental well-being. The ability to accept immutable life circumstances allows a person to focus their energy on how they react to those circumstances, rather than fixating on the inevitable.

Seeking social support:
- People tend to seek social support, whether it's by talking to friends or family, sharing experiences, or seeking professional help. Social support can have a significant impact on coping.

Avoidance and withdrawal:
- Some people tend to avoid stressful situations or withdraw to reduce their stress. However, this can have both adaptive and maladaptive effects.

Coping Styles:

- There are different coping styles that people typically use. Some prefer active coping, while others are more likely to resort to passive strategies. Individual differences may be due to personality, experiences, and contextual factors.

Long-term coping and resilience:

- Resilience refers to the ability to recover from stress and emerge stronger. Effective coping helps to promote resilience and deal with challenges in the long term.

Cognitive Processing:

- Coping also includes cognitive processes, such as the way people interpret a situation, regulate their thoughts, and deal with stress-inducing beliefs.

Culture and Coping:

- Coping strategies can be culturally influenced. Different cultures may have different ideas about appropriate coping mechanisms.

Coping is individual, and what works for one person may not work for another. The ability to develop healthy coping strategies is an important aspect of mental health and well-being.

Couples Counseling/Relationship Counseling

Couples counseling is a form of psychosocial counseling that helps couples improve their relationship, manage conflict, and strengthen their communication skills. Couples counseling can be provided by various professionals such as psychologists, therapists, social workers, or marriage counselors.

Communication Improvement:
- A common goal of couples counseling is to improve communication between partners. This includes learning effective communication techniques, listening, and expressing needs and feelings.

Conflict resolution:
- Couples counseling supports couples in managing conflicts constructively. This includes understanding the causes of conflict, learning conflict resolution strategies, and developing compromise skills.

Relationship Strengthening:
- Couples counseling focuses on strengthening the existing relationship. This can be achieved by recognising and promoting positive aspects of the partnership as well as jointly developing goals and values.

Understanding Partner Dynamics:
- Therapists in couples counseling help partners understand the dynamics of their relationship. This may include identifying patterns in communication or behaviors that lead to problems.

Promote intimacy and closeness:
- Couples counseling can help promote intimacy and closeness in the relationship. This can be done by creating

emotional connection, reviving romantic elements, and developing shared activities.

Coping with life changes:
- Couples counseling is often helpful in coping with life changes, such as the birth of a child, career changes, the loss of a loved one, or other stressors.

Support for sexual problems:
- Couples counseling can also address and support sexual issues, whether that's by disclosing sexual needs, managing disagreements, or exploring new ways to improve intimacy.

Fostering Emotional Intelligence:
- Couples counseling can help strengthen partners' emotional intelligence by helping them understand their own emotions and respond appropriately to the partner's emotions.

Preparation for marriage or civil partnership:
- Sometimes, couples seek help before marriage or moving in together to prepare for the challenges of living together. Couples counseling can help set realistic expectations and build a strong foundation for the future together.

Resources for dealing with difficulties:
- Couples counseling also provides partners with resources and tools to deal with future difficulties on their own. This often involves developing strategies to maintain a healthy relationship over the long term.

It is important that couples counseling is individually tailored to the needs and goals of each couple. It provides a supportive space where couples can learn to grow together and overcome challenges together.

Crisis intervention

Crisis intervention refers to short-term, intensive measures to support people in acute psychological, emotional or social crisis situations. The aim of crisis intervention is to offer immediate help to prevent further deterioration and to prepare those affected for a more stable situation.

Quick Response:
- Crisis intervention requires a quick and timely response to the acute situation. The support should be provided immediately after the onset of the crisis.

Clarification of the situation:
- The crisis intervenor tries to clarify the situation and understand the specific challenges and needs of the affected person.

Assessment of the security risk:
- A safety risk assessment is crucial to ensure that there is no imminent threat to life or physical integrity.

Emotional Support:
- Crisis intervention involves the provision of emotional support. This can include listening, understanding, and showing empathy.

Coping:
- Coping strategies are developed together with the person concerned. These can be practical steps to solve problems or reduce stress.

Availability:
- Crisis intervenors should be available to the person concerned. This can be done through telephone contacts, face-to-face meetings, or other means of communication.

Provide information:

- The data subject should be provided with relevant information, whether about available resources, support services, or further steps that can be taken.

Recommendations for professional help:

- In some cases, it may be necessary to recommend professional help from psychologists, psychiatrists, or other health care providers. The crisis intervenor can support the affected person in finding suitable resources.

Promote self-care:

- Crisis intervention also includes the promotion of self-care. The affected person is encouraged to take care of their own health and well-being.

Maintain confidentiality:

- It is important to maintain confidentiality and ensure that the person feels safe to talk openly about their situation.

Collaboration with other professionals:

- In complex cases, it may be necessary to work with other professionals or organizations to ensure comprehensive support.

Follow-up:

- After crisis intervention, follow-up is important. This may mean engaging with the affected person on a regular basis to ensure that they receive appropriate support.

Crisis intervention is not a long-term therapy, but focuses on the immediate needs and interventions to support people in acute crisis situations. Professional crisis intervention assistants can work in a variety of fields, such as psychological counseling, social work, emergency services, and health care.

Crisis management

Crisis management refers to the process of dealing with unexpected and challenging situations in order to minimize their impact and promote the most positive coping possible. Crises can occur in different areas of life: personal, professional, health, social or global.

Early diagnosis:
- Early detection of crises is crucial. The timely detection of signs and signals makes it possible to take preventive measures and prevent or mitigate the escalation of the crisis.

Crisis Management Plan:
- Developing a crisis management plan is an important step. This plan should include clear responsibilities, courses of action, and communication strategies to respond effectively to the crisis.

Communication:
- Open and transparent communication is crucial. Affected parties must be informed of the situation, the actions that will be taken and the expected changes in order to minimize uncertainty.

Resource Mobilization:
- Identifying and mobilising resources, be it human resources, finances or technological means, is an important part of crisis management. This ensures the effective implementation of measures.

Psychosocial support:
- Crises can cause significant emotional stress. Providing psychosocial support to those affected and those involved is important to deal with the emotional impact.

Flexibility and adaptability:

- In times of crisis, flexibility is crucial. Plans need to be adjusted as needed to respond to changing circumstances and unpredictable developments.

Learning from experience:

- After overcoming a crisis, it is important to conduct a retrospective analysis. Gaining experience and identifying opportunities for improvement will help you be better prepared for future crises.

Collaboration and networking:

- In many crisis situations, close cooperation with other organizations, institutions or communities is required. The formation of networks and partnerships strengthens the overall capacity to deal with crises.

Long-term perspective:

- Crisis management should not only take place in the short term, but also take into account long-term perspectives. This includes restoring communities, rebuilding, and creating more resilient systems.

Prevention:

- Crisis management should be accompanied by an emphasis on risk prevention. Identifying potential risks and implementing risk mitigation strategies will help minimize future crises.

Crisis:

- A special focus should be on crisis communication. Clear, concise and regular communication with all stakeholders involved is crucial for dealing with uncertainty and fears.

Self-Care:

- Emphasizing self-care, both for individuals and organizations, is important. The ability to support oneself and provide for well-being contributes to long-term resilience.

Crisis management requires comprehensive and coordinated efforts at various levels. This is not only about responding to a crisis immediately, but also about strengthening the resilience of communities and organizations to future challenges.

Cultural sensitivity

Cultural sensitivity refers to the ability to recognize, understand, and respond appropriately to cultural differences. It is of great importance in various areas, especially in the areas of social affairs, health and education.

Recognition of cultural diversity:
- Cultural sensitivity begins with the recognition and appreciation of cultural diversity. It is important to understand that people have different backgrounds, values, norms, and practices.

Respect for cultural differences:
- Respect for other cultures is key. This includes respecting cultural identity and avoiding prejudice or stereotypes.

Self-reflection:
- Cultural sensitivity requires self-reflection. People should be aware of their own cultural backgrounds, values, and biases in order to better understand their interactions with others.

Intercultural Communication:
- The ability to communicate interculturally is crucial. This includes not only verbal communication, but also understanding non-verbal signals and cultural nuances.

Empathy:

- Empathy, empathizing with the perspectives and feelings of others, is an essential part of cultural sensitivity. This allows for a deeper understanding of other people's experiences.

Adaptability:

- Culturally sensitive people are flexible and adaptable in different cultural contexts. They acknowledge that different situations may require different cultural approaches.

Culturally sensitive services:

- In professional fields, such as healthcare, education or social work, services should be designed to be culturally sensitive. This means taking into account the needs and preferences of different cultures.

Avoidance of stereotypes:

- Culturally sensitive people avoid using or promoting stereotypes. They recognize that individual differences within a culture are just as important as similarities.

Education and awareness-raising:

- Ongoing education and awareness of cultural diversity are important. This may include training, workshops, or learning resources to deepen understanding.

Collaboration and participation:

- Culturally sensitive practices promote collaboration and participation of all stakeholders, regardless of their cultural affiliation. This reinforces the inclusive nature of organizations and communities.

Cultural Competence:

- The development of cultural competence, i.e. the ability to act effectively in different cultural contexts, is a goal of cultural sensitivity.

Responding to cultural needs:

- Culturally sensitive practices include the ability to respond appropriately to specific cultural needs and concerns. This may include individual adaptations of services or interventions.

Fostering cultural sensitivity helps create an inclusive and respectful environment where people are treated equally regardless of their cultural background. This is especially important in societies that are becoming increasingly diverse.

Debt counselling

Debt counselling is an area of social work that focuses on supporting people with financial difficulties or debt problems. The main goal of debt counselling is to help those affected to improve their financial situation, reduce debt and achieve a stable financial situation in the long term.

Financial analysis:
- As a first step, debt counsellors conduct a comprehensive financial analysis to understand the client's exact financial situation. This includes recording all sources of income, expenses, debts, and assets.

Budget:
- Based on the financial analysis, debt counselling supports clients in creating a realistic budget. The aim is to balance income and expenditure while creating enough leeway for debt repayment.

Negotiations with creditors:
- Debt counselors can enter into negotiations with creditors to agree on payment schedules, reduce interest, or make other arrangements that reduce the financial burden on the debtor.

Information and education:

- Debt counselling also includes the provision of information and education on financial matters. This may include training on financial literacy, debt management, and consumer rights.

Mediation of support services:

- Debt counselors can assist clients in taking advantage of government assistance services or other financial assistance programs to stabilize their financial situation.

Prevention of re-indebtedness:

- In addition to managing existing debts, debt counseling aims to develop strategies to prevent re-indebtedness. This can include promoting responsible money stewardship and developing long-term financial goals.

Psychosocial support:

- Financial problems can cause significant stress and emotional distress. Debt counselling, therefore, also provides psychosocial support to help deal with the emotional impact of debt and help clients strengthen their stress management skills.

Long-term support:

- Debt counseling may also include long-term support to ensure clients achieve and maintain their financial goals. This may include regular reviews of the budget and progress.

Debt counselling is an important service that helps to help people out of financial crises and provide them with the tools and knowledge to achieve sustainable financial health.

Deinstitutionalization

Deinstitutionalization is a social policy approach that aims to release people with mental illness or intellectual disabilities from institutionalized institutions such as psychiatric hospitals or nursing homes and reintegrate them into the community. This approach has been implemented to varying degrees in different countries, with different challenges and successes.

Background:
- Deinstitutionalization was introduced in the 1960s and 1970s in response to abuses in some psychiatric institutions. These facilities have often been criticized for their poor living conditions, overcrowding, and lack of individualized treatment approaches.

Goal:
- The main goal of deinstitutionalization is to reintegrate people with mental illness into society and allow them to live as normal a life as possible in their community.

Community-Based Care:
- A key aspect of deinstitutionalization is the introduction of community-based utilities. This includes outpatient mental health services, assisted living, day centers, and other resources in the community.

Normalization:
- Normalization is a concept associated with deinstitutionalization that aims to allow people with mental illness to live as normal a life as possible. This includes access to education, work, leisure activities and social relationships.

Implementation challenges:

- The implementation of deinstitutionalisation has presented challenges in some cases. These include potential deficiencies in funding for community services, the need for adequate housing and support services, and the stigma of people with mental illness in the community.

Criticism:

- Deinstitutionalization has also been criticized, especially when it is not accompanied by adequate support and community services. This can lead to homelessness, incarceration, or a lack of adequate care.

Developments in the field of psychopharmacology:

- Advances in psychopharmacology have also had an impact on deinstitutionalization, as drug therapies allow many people to live outside of institutions.

Reforms in the field of jurisprudence:

- In some countries, legal reforms have helped to strengthen the rights of people with mental illness and create the conditions for successful deinstitutionalization.

Need for long-term support:

- Successful deinstitutionalization often requires long-term support services, including regular monitoring, medical care, and psychosocial support.

Variations in implementation:

- The implementation of deinstitutionalization varies significantly around the world and is influenced by cultural, political, and financial factors.

Deinstitutionalization has helped improve the quality of life of many people with mental illness, but remains a complex socio-policy challenge that requires careful planning and resources.

Disability law

Disability law comprises legal norms and regulations aimed at protecting the rights of persons with disabilities, promoting their participation in society and preventing discrimination. There are national and international legal instruments that shape disability law.

International level:
UN Convention on the Rights of Persons with Disabilities (UNCRPD): This is an international human rights treaty of the United Nations that protects the rights of persons with disabilities and promotes their equal participation in all areas of life. The CRPD emphasizes the principles of non-discrimination, inclusion and self-determination.

National implementation:
- In many countries, the principles of the CRPD are transposed into national law. This can be done through specific disability equality laws or more general anti-discrimination laws.

Equality and non-discrimination:
- Disability law strives for equality for people with disabilities. This means that they should have the same rights and opportunities as people without disabilities. In addition, discrimination on the basis of disability is to be prevented.

Accessibility:
- Disability law emphasizes the importance of accessibility in various areas of life, including public spaces, buildings, transport, communication, and the digital environment. Accessibility is intended to ensure that people with disabilities can participate fully in social life.

Participation in the labour market:
- People with disabilities have the right to work and should have equal access to the labour market. In many countries, job adaptations and support services are regulated by disability law.

Education:
- The right to education for persons with disabilities is emphasized in disability law. This includes access to inclusive education and appropriate support measures.

Health care:
- Disability law also addresses access to health care and supportive therapies for people with disabilities.

Self-determination and autonomy:
- The right to self-determination and autonomy is a central principle of disability law. This means that people with disabilities can make their own decisions and live their lives on their own terms.

Special protective measures:
- In some cases, disability law provides for specific safeguards to ensure that people with severe or complex disabilities are adequately supported.

Right to Appeal and Enforcement:
- Disability rights should include mechanisms for complaints and enforcement so that people with disabilities can assert their rights.

Disability law serves to ensure the participation and dignity of persons with disabilities in society and to ensure that their needs are adequately addressed. It is constantly evolving to meet changing needs and insights.

Disability pension

The disability pension is a form of pension that is no longer able to work fully or at all due to health restrictions or disabilities. Basic information about the Disability pension is:

Health check:
- As a rule, the granting of a disability pension is determined by a health examination. A medical report or medical records are often needed to assess the nature and degree of health impairment.

Degree of disability:
- The degree of disability plays a central role in deciding on the amount of the pension. This degree is often expressed as a percentage and reflects the extent to which the ability to work is impaired.

Periods:
- Applicants must provide proof of a certain number of insurance periods in order to be eligible for a full disability pension. These periods may relate to previous contributions to pension insurance or similar schemes.

Fixed-term or permanent pension:
- The disability pension can be granted for a limited or unlimited period, depending on the assessment of the chances of recovery and the possibility of returning to work in the foreseeable future.

Partial or total disability:
- There are often distinctions between partial and full disability. In the case of partial disability, the person may still be able to work to a limited extent, while in the case of a total disability, the ability to work is significantly reduced.

Rehabilitation:
- Vocational rehabilitation measures may be part of the disability pension scheme. This may include, for example, training or support for professional reintegration.

Income imputation:
- In some schemes, the amount of the disability pension may depend on other incomes. This means that other income can affect pension payments.

-

Application Process:
- Applying for a disability pension often requires a formal application, which must be submitted with relevant medical documentation. An appraisal by a pension insurance institution or an appraiser may also be required.

Diversity

Diversity refers to the diversity and diversity of people in a particular group, organization, or community. This diversity can manifest itself in many ways, including but not limited to ethnicity, gender, age, sexual orientation, religion, disability, socioeconomic status, and more. The recognition and appreciation of diversity are central elements in many social, cultural and organizational contexts.

Inclusion:
- Inclusion is closely related to diversity and refers to how diversity is actively promoted and integrated into all aspects of a group or organization. It's about creating an

environment where all members feel respected, accepted, and involved.

Dimensions of diversity:

- Diversity spans various dimensions, including ethnicity, gender, sexual orientation, age, religion, physical and mental abilities, socioeconomic status, educational background, and more.

Benefits of diversity:

- Diversity is often seen as a strength. Different perspectives and experiences can contribute to creative solutions, innovative thinking, and a productive work environment. Diversity can also increase the performance and engagement of a group's members.

Challenges and conflicts:

- Despite the benefits, diversity and inclusion can also present challenges. Differing views and values can lead to conflict, and it is important to establish mechanisms for conflict resolution and communication.

Awareness:

- Educational initiatives and training can help raise awareness of the importance of diversity and counteract stereotypes and prejudices.

Representation:

- Representation in different contexts, such as the media, corporate boardrooms or political bodies, plays an important role in creating an inclusive society.

Legal framework:

- In some countries, there are legal provisions and policies that support the promotion of diversity and the prevention of discrimination. These include anti-discrimination laws and measures to promote equal opportunities.

Cultural Sensitivity:

- Developing cultural sensitivity and intercultural skills is crucial to respectfully dealing with different backgrounds.

Affirmative Action:
- In some contexts, affirmative measures are taken to support historically disadvantaged groups and improve access to education, employment, and other resources.

Global Perspective:
- Diversity also has a global dimension, as people from different parts of the world interact with each other. Intercultural cooperation and the recognition of global diversity are of great importance in an interconnected world.

Promoting diversity and inclusion is not only an ethical commitment, but also a strategic choice that has the potential to foster creative dynamism and innovation in various fields.

Dual mandate

The "dual mandate" refers to an organization's simultaneous commitment to pursue both economic and social goals. This idea is related to Corporate Social Responsibility (CSR) and concerns the question of whether companies should not only be profit-oriented, but should also adopt social and environmental responsibility.

Economic objectives:
- The economic mandate refers to the traditional role of companies in generating profits and maximizing shareholder value. It emphasizes a company's obligation to its owners and shareholders to generate profits.

Social Goals:

- The social mandate refers to a company's responsibility to society and emphasizes that companies should not only aim for economic success, but also create social added value. This may relate to social justice, environmental protection, ethical business conduct, and other societal concerns.

Criticism of the dual mandate:

- Critics of the dual mandate argue that by focusing on social responsibility, companies could potentially neglect their main mission, which is economic success. This could lead to a lack of competitiveness and financial stability.

Integration of economic and social affairs:

- Proponents of the dual mandate argue that economic and social goals do not necessarily have to conflict with each other. Rather, they could be integrated to promote long-term sustainability and a positive contribution to society.

Corporate Social Responsibility (CSR):

- The dual mandate is in line with the concept of Corporate Social Responsibility (CSR), in which companies design their activities in such a way that they pursue both economic benefits and social and environmental objectives.

Long-term perspective:

- The dual mandate often emphasizes a long-term perspective that goes beyond short-term profit maximization. Companies that adopt social responsibility could see long-term benefits in terms of customer loyalty, employee retention, and company reputation.

Societal expectations:

- Society's expectations of companies have changed, and companies are increasingly expected to assume their social and environmental responsibilities. The dual mandate reflects these changing expectations.

UN Sustainable Development Goals (SDGs):
- The dual mandate may also be linked to the UN Sustainable Development Goals (SDGs), which encompass a number of global goals for sustainable development, including poverty eradication, gender equality, clean water, and affordable and clean energy.

Companies with a dual mandate try to find a balanced approach that takes into account both economic and social concerns. The discussion on the dual mandate is part of a wider dialogue on the role of businesses in society and how they can make a positive contribution to the common good.

Early Childhood Education

Early childhood education deals with the upbringing and education of children in the first years of life, especially in early childhood. The focus is on the holistic development of the child, which includes cognitive, emotional, social and motor aspects. Early childhood education is not only focused on imparting knowledge, but also emphasizes the promotion of social skills, emotional intelligence, and creative expression.

Holistic approach:
- Early childhood education takes a holistic approach that supports children's comprehensive development in the areas of cognition, motor skills, language, social behavior, and emotional intelligence.

Sensitive handling of children:

- Early childhood education emphasizes a sensitive and respectful approach to children. Educators take into account the needs and personalities of each child.

Early promotion of key competences:

- Early childhood education aims to promote key competencies such as language development, social interaction, fine and gross motor skills, and cognitive skills from the very beginning.

Participation and self-determination:

- Children are encouraged to actively participate in their own development and to express their interests, abilities and needs. Self-determination and personal responsibility are supported.

Inclusion:

- Early childhood education is inclusive and is aimed at all children regardless of their abilities, backgrounds or special needs. The aim is to create optimal learning opportunities for each child.

Parent Partnership:

- Cooperation with parents is a central aspect of early childhood education. Educators and parents work together to understand the child's individual needs and create supportive learning environments.

Play as a form of learning:

- Play is seen as a central form of learning. Through play, children develop cognitive skills, social skills, and creative expression.

Cultural Sensitivity:

- Early childhood education takes into account the cultural diversity of children and promotes cultural sensitivity and interaction in the learning environment.

Development of basic skills:

- Basic competencies such as emotional intelligence, self-regulation, social skills and problem-solving skills are the focus of early childhood education.

Relationship building:

- Creating positive relationships between educators, children and parents is a fundamental aspect of early childhood education. Relationships form the basis of a supportive learning environment.

Preparing for school:

- Early childhood education prepares children for the transition to school by promoting the development of basic skills and a positive attitude towards learning.

Early childhood education is important at the stage of life when children develop basic skills, attitudes, and social skills. High-quality early childhood education lays the foundation for lifelong learning and positive developmental trajectories.

Early Intervention

Early intervention refers to measures and programmes that aim to promote the development of children in the first years of life and to identify and treat possible developmental delays or impairments at an early stage. The aim is to provide children with an optimal basis for their cognitive, emotional, social and motor development.

Aim of early intervention:
- The main goal of early intervention is to provide comprehensive support for children's development in order to identify possible developmental delays or impairments at an early stage and to initiate targeted support measures.

Early detection and intervention:
- Early intervention involves early identification of developmental risks or delays, as well as timely intervention to fully develop children's potential.

Interdisciplinary approach:
- Early intervention is often provided by an interdisciplinary team of professionals, including educators, psychologists, occupational therapists, speech therapists, physical therapists, and other specialists, depending on the child's needs.

Parental involvement:
- Parental involvement is an essential part of early childhood education. Parents are actively involved in the process in order to support the support measures and strengthen parental competence.

Promotion of key competences:
- Early intervention focuses on promoting key competencies such as language development, fine and gross motor skills, social interaction, and cognitive skills.

Individualized support:
- Each child is considered individually, and support measures are developed according to the child's specific needs and strengths.

Inclusive approach:
- Early intervention takes an inclusive approach that ensures children from diverse abilities and backgrounds receive the support they need to learn and develop successfully.

Early intervention in various areas:

- Early intervention can take place in a variety of areas, including motor development, cognitive development, social-emotional development, and language development.
Support transitions:
- Early intervention plays an important role in supporting children during transitions, such as the transition from early intervention to preschool or from preschool to primary school.
Early intervention for risk factors:
- In some cases, early intervention is particularly intensive when children are exposed to certain risk factors, such as prematurity, genetic factors or environmental stresses.

Early intervention is crucial to ensure that children have optimal development opportunities and challenges are addressed early to minimise long-term impacts. It is a holistic approach that takes into account the needs of the child and his family.

Educational Aids

"Educational assistance" is a term used in child and youth welfare that includes various measures and support services to ensure the well-being of children and young people. As a rule, these aids are used when the child's well-being is endangered or when particular difficulties arise in the upbringing.

Outpatient aids:

- Outpatient parenting services are usually offered in the home environment of the child or adolescent. These include, for example, educational counselling, family therapy or socio-educational support.

Semi-inpatient aids:

- Partial inpatient assistance means that the child or adolescent is temporarily cared for outside the parental home. These include, for example, day groups or socio-educational institutions.

Inpatient aids:

- Inpatient assistance means that the child or adolescent is placed completely outside the parental home in an inpatient facility. This can be done in foster families, homes or group homes.

Bringing up in another family:

- If placement with the family of origin is not possible or is not in the best interests of the child, placement with a foster family or adoptive family can take place.

Therapeutic measures:

- Parenting aids may include therapeutic interventions to treat specific problems or behavioural problems in children or adolescents. This may include psychological therapy, psychotherapy, or other therapeutic approaches.

Educational support:

- Promoting school development is an important aspect. This can be done through tutoring, remedial teaching or special pedagogical measures.

Parenting:

- Involving parents in the help process is crucial. This includes parent training, parenting counselling and measures aimed at strengthening parents' parenting skills.

Leisure and educational activities:

- Participation in leisure and educational activities helps to promote social integration and personal development. This may include sports activities, cultural offerings or other leisure activities.

Help with coping with life:
- Parenting assistance can also provide support in coping with everyday life demands, including financial support and help in organizing everyday life.

Child protection:
- Child protection is an important aspect of educational support. This includes measures to protect children from neglect, abuse or other forms of vulnerability.

The aim of educational support is to take into account the individual needs and rights of children and young people and to enable them to grow up safely, supportively and supportively. The use of this aid is carried out in close cooperation with the affected families and with the participation of the children and young people themselves.

Emancipation

Emancipation refers to the process of liberation from oppression, paternalism or restriction, especially through social norms, gender roles or political systems. The term is used in various contexts and can refer to individual, social, political or economic emancipation.

Gender emancipation:
- In terms of gender roles, emancipation refers to the process by which women and other marginalized genders are

liberated from traditional social, political, and economic constraints. This includes access to education, job opportunities and political participation.

Individual emancipation:

- On an individual level, emancipation can mean that a person frees himself from personal limitations or dependencies and leads a self-determined life. This can take place in various areas of life, including personal relationships, education, and professional development.

Social Emancipation:

- Social emancipation refers to certain social groups expanding their rights and opportunities to achieve equality and social justice. This can refer to ethnic groups, LGBTQ+ communities, people with disabilities, and other groups.

Political Emancipation:

- Political emancipation involves liberation from political oppression and participation in political decision-making processes. This may include access to civic education, the right to vote, and the opportunity to engage in politics.

Economic emancipation:

- Economic emancipation refers to liberation from economic dependence and poverty. This can be achieved through access to job opportunities, fair wages, entrepreneurial opportunities, and economic education.

Cultural Emancipation:

- Cultural emancipation refers to breaking free from cultural norms and stereotypes that marginalize or limit certain groups. This can concern cultural diversity, cultural identity and cultural recognition.

Education as the key:

- Education often plays a key role in emancipation. Access to education allows people to develop their skills, foster critical thinking, and improve their chances of emancipation in various areas of life.

Self-determination:

- Self-determination is a central element of emancipation. It's about individuals and groups being in control of their own lives and choices.

Legal and political framework:

- The creation of legal and political frameworks that guarantee the equality and freedom of all citizens is crucial for emancipation.

Ongoing Process:

- Emancipation is often an ongoing process that requires both individual and societal changes. It's about breaking down barriers, creating awareness, and fighting for change at different levels.

Emancipation is a dynamic and multi-layered process that promotes the development of individual and collective autonomy and freedom. It is a central concept of many social movements working to eliminate inequality and discrimination.

Empathy

Empathy is the ability to understand and emotionally comprehend other people's feelings, thoughts, and perspectives. It goes beyond simply recognizing emotions and involves deep empathy with the experiences of others. Empathy plays a crucial role in interpersonal relationships, communication, and social behavior.

Empathy vs. Sympathy:

- Empathy is sometimes confused with sympathy. While sympathy involves compassion for the suffering of others, empathy goes beyond that and involves understanding and feeling another person's emotions.

Empathetic Understanding:

- Empathy involves an empathetic understanding of the feelings and perspectives of others, even if they are different from one's own.

Cognitive Empathy:

- Cognitive empathy refers to the ability to understand the perspectives and thoughts of others. It requires the ability to take on perspectives and change perspectives.

Emotional empathy:

- Emotional empathy refers to the ability to feel the emotional states of others. It makes it possible to empathize with a person's emotions and share their feelings.

Empathy in communication:

- In communication, empathy is important to create an effective interpersonal connection. Empathetic communication signals that the feelings and perspectives of the interlocutor are perceived and respected.

Social Empathy:

- Social empathy refers to the ability to understand social dynamics and expectations. This is especially important in group or team interactions.

Development aspect:

- The capacity for empathy develops over the course of life. Especially in childhood and adolescence, the development of empathy is an important part of social learning.

Empathy in the nursing professions:

- In nursing, medical and other helping professions, empathy is of central importance. The ability to empathize with the situation and feelings of patients or clients contributes to high-quality care.

Limits of empathy:

- There are limits to empathy, especially when it comes to understanding experiences that are very different from one's own. Still, empathetic behavior can be helpful even if you can't understand all aspects of the experience.

Fostering empathy and compassion:

- Empathy can be fostered through conscious listening, perspective-taking, mindfulness, and a willingness to self-reflect.

Empathy plays a key role in interpersonal relationships, conflict resolution, social cohesion, and the development of compassion and understanding of the diversity of human experiences.

Empowerment

Empowerment refers to the process of empowering individuals or groups to take control of their lives, make decisions, and influence those around them. The term is used in various contexts, including social work, education, health, politics, and corporate governance.

Self-determination:

- Empowerment emphasizes the promotion of self-determination. It aims to give people the ability to make their own decisions and influence their living conditions.

Empowering individuals and groups:
- Empowerment can refer to individuals or groups. It involves empowering people, regardless of gender, age, social background, or other characteristics.

Participation:
- Participation is a central element of empowerment. This refers to the active participation of individuals or groups in decision-making processes that affect their lives.

Education and Awareness:
- Empowerment often involves education and awareness-raising. Providing knowledge and information enables people to make informed decisions and increase their ability to act.

Skills Development:
- Developing skills and competencies is an essential part of empowerment. This can include both formal education and the promotion of practical skills.

Access to resources:
- Empowerment also involves access to resources, whether related to education, employment, health care, or other areas that affect quality of life.

Critical Reflection:
- Critical reflection on social structures and power relations is another aspect of empowerment. It's about identifying and addressing inequalities and barriers.

Self-efficacy:
- Self-efficacy, confidence in one's own ability to bring about change, is a key concept in empowerment. It fosters the feeling that individual action can have an impact.

Justice and Equality:
- Empowerment strives for justice and equality. This includes recognising diversity and eliminating discrimination.

Sustainability:

- Sustainability is an important goal of empowerment. It's about creating changes that have a long-term positive impact, not just short-term improvements.

Empowerment is a proactive approach that aims to equip people with the means and resources they need to improve their living conditions and actively participate in shaping their own destiny. Empowerment plays a crucial role in promoting equality, social justice and sustainable development.

Endangering the well-being of children

Child endangerment refers to situations in which the physical, emotional, or mental well-being of a child or adolescent is at risk. This can be caused by various forms of neglect, abuse, or other threats.

Definition:

- Endangerment of the child's well-being exists when the physical, emotional or mental well-being of a child is significantly impaired or threatened. This can be caused by neglect, physical or emotional abuse, sexual abuse, or other harmful acts.

Forms of child endangerment:

- Endangerment of the child's well-being can come in a variety of forms, including physical neglect, emotional neglect, physical abuse, sexual abuse, psychological abuse, or witnessing domestic violence.

Indicators of child endangerment:

- Signs of potential child endangerment may include abnormal behavior of the child, physical injuries, emotional problems, neglect of basic needs, unusual changes in behavior, or regular absenteeism from school.

Notification and Protection:

- In many countries, health, education and social work professionals are required by law to report suspected child endangerment. The goal is to protect the child from further harm and to offer support to the family.

Child protection measures:

- If a child's well-being is suspected, various child protection measures can be taken. These include interim protection measures, family court orders, therapy services and counselling services.

Family support:

- The protection of the child's best interests often includes the support of the family. Measures can be taken to help parents overcome challenges and ensure that the child grows up in a safe environment.

Early detection and prevention:

- Early detection of risk factors and preventive measures play an important role in child protection. These include parent education programmes, early detection examinations and offers to strengthen parental skills.

Interdisciplinary cooperation:

- Child protection often requires the cooperation of different disciplines, including health, education, social work and the judiciary. Interdisciplinary teams can help ensure comprehensive and coordinated support.

Legal framework:

- Many countries have legal frameworks and child protection laws that govern the protection of children at risk. These laws specify what measures can be taken to ensure the best interests of the child.

Aftercare and monitoring:
- After an intervention, continuous follow-up and monitoring is important to ensure that the risk to the child's well-being is minimized in the long term.

Child endangerment is a serious matter that requires a quick and coordinated response to protect the child's best interests and ensure supportive measures for the family.

Ethics

Ethics is the systematic reflection on moral principles and values, as well as the evaluation of actions and decisions in terms of their moral justification. It is a branch of philosophy that deals with questions of morality and the principles that guide the behavior of individuals, groups, or institutions.

Morals and Ethics:
- The term "morality" is often used interchangeably with "ethics." Morality refers to people's actual actions, decisions, and behaviors, while ethics is the systematic study of the principles and values that underpin those actions.

Normative Ethics:
- Normative ethics is concerned with the development of ethical theories and principles that serve as a guide for

moral action. Examples include deontological ethics, consequentialist ethics, and virtue ethics.

Applied Ethics:
- Applied ethics refers to the application of ethical principles to concrete situations and issues in various fields such as medicine, science, business, environmental protection, and technology.

Metaethics:
- Metaethics looks at fundamental questions about what morality actually is. She examines concepts such as truth, meaning, and objectivity in relation to moral statements.

Individual Ethics:
- Individual ethics refers to an individual's personal moral beliefs and values that influence their behavior and decisions.

Social Ethics:
- Social ethics concerns the moral principles that guide the behavior of groups, societies, or institutions. This can relate to issues of justice, human rights and social responsibility.

Professionalism and Ethics:
- Many professions have ethical guidelines and codes of conduct that are designed to ensure that professionals act in accordance with moral principles.

Cultural relativity:
- Ethics can be culturally variable, and cultural relativity refers to the idea that moral principles can be different in different cultures.

Ethics in Technology and AI:
- With the advancement of technology and artificial intelligence, ethical issues arise regarding privacy, automation, accountability of algorithms, and the use of technology in various areas of life.

Responsibility and Ethics:
- Ethics often emphasizes the idea of responsibility, whether it be personal responsibility for individual actions or the

responsibility of organizations and societies for their impact on the world.

Ethics plays a central role in human coexistence and social order. It provides a framework for evaluating actions, promoting moral reflection, and building trust and cooperation in different social contexts.

Ethnicity

Ethnicity refers to belonging to a particular social group based on common cultural characteristics such as language, religion, traditions, customs and customs, and often on common ancestry or regional origin. It is essential that ethnicity is not the same as race, although these terms are sometimes confused. Ethnicity is more culturally and socially constructed, while race often has biological or genetic connotations.

Cultural identity:
- Ethnicity plays an important role in constructing the cultural identity of a group or individual. The common cultural characteristics can form the basis for identification with a particular ethnic group.

Common origin:
- Ethnicity is often associated with common ancestry or ancestry. People in an ethnic group may share a common history, origins, or migration experiences.

Language and Communication:

- The common language is often a central element of ethnic identity. The way a group communicates can reflect their belonging to a particular ethnic community.

Religion and customs:

- Religion and customs also play a role in defining ethnicity. Shared religious beliefs and rituals can bind members of an ethnic group together.

Shared values:

- Ethnic groups may have shared values and norms that influence their social interactions and the way they live together.

Diversity within ethnic groups:

- It should be noted that ethnic groups are often internally diverse. There are often differences in terms of dialects, regional differences, socioeconomic status, and other factors within an ethnic group.

Ethnicity and Nation:

- Ethnicity and nationality are different concepts. While ethnicity refers to cultural commonalities, nationality refers to belonging to a political entity.

Ethnic conflicts:

- In some cases, ethnic differences can lead to tension or conflict, especially when political, economic, or social resources are at stake.

Self-identification:

- Belonging to an ethnic group is often a matter of self-identification. Individuals may or may not assign themselves to a particular ethnic group, depending on personal beliefs and experiences.

Multiculturalism:

- In societies that are multicultural, the diversity of ethnicities is often seen as an enrichment. Multiculturalism refers to the recognition and acceptance of different cultural backgrounds.

It should be emphasized that ethnicity is a socially constructed concept and that the definition and meaning of ethnicity can vary in different cultures and contexts.

Evaluation/Evaluation

Evaluation is the systematic process of collecting, analyzing, and interpreting information to assess the value, benefit, or effectiveness of a project, program, policy, or intervention. The aim of the evaluation is to gain insights into the extent to which the set goals have been achieved, what effects a measure has had and how implementation can be improved.

Objectives of the evaluation:
- The objectives of the evaluation are set at the beginning of the process and may vary depending on the context. It could be about assessing the effectiveness, efficiency, relevance, sustainability or benefits of a measure.

Evaluation types:
- There are several types of evaluations, including formative evaluation (during development for improvement), summative evaluation (after completion for overall evaluation), and formive-summative approach (a combination of both).

Indicators and metrics:
- In order to assess effectiveness, clear indicators and metrics are established. These can include quantitative (e.g. figures, statistics) or qualitative (e.g. testimonials, interviews) data.

Logic Model:

- A logic model or impact model is often created to represent the assumptions and relationships between activities, outcomes, and long-term goals of an intervention.

Data collection methods:

- Various methods of data collection are used, including surveys, interviews, focus groups, observations, and analysis of documents. The choice depends on the objectives of the evaluation and the resources available.

Participation of stakeholders:

- Stakeholders, including target groups, decision-makers and other stakeholders, are often involved in the evaluation process to consider different perspectives.

Cultural Competence:

- Cultural competence is important, especially in international or culturally diverse contexts, to ensure that evaluation is carried out appropriately and sensitively.

Usefulness and applicability:

- A good evaluation should not only be accurate and reliable, but also provide useful insights that are relevant for improving the measure or for future decisions.

Ethics in Evaluation:

- Ethics plays an important role, especially in terms of the protection of participants, the confidentiality of data and the transparent communication of results.

Continuous Improvement:

- The evaluation process itself can contribute to continuous improvement by integrating feedback mechanisms and learning processes.

Use of results:

- A central aspect of the evaluation is the use of results. The results should be actively used to inform decisions, optimize programs, or drive policy change.

Evaluation is crucial in various fields such as education, health, social work, development cooperation and corporate governance. A well-conducted evaluation can help to use resources more efficiently, maximise the benefits for the target groups and improve the quality of programmes and measures.

Family Assistance

Family assistance is a support service that aims to help families in different life situations, improve their quality of life and strengthen the skills of family members. This support can be provided by professionals, social workers or family helpers.

Objectives of Family Assistance:
- The goals of family support vary according to the needs of the family, but may include fostering parenting skills, managing crises, improving family relationships, and creating a safe and supportive environment.

Early intervention:
- Family support can be used in a variety of life situations, including early intervention to identify and manage potential problems before they develop into more serious challenges.

Support with parenting issues:
- An important aspect of family support is to help parents develop their parenting skills. This may include promoting

positive parenting methods, managing behavioral problems, and improving family communication.

Crisis management:
- Family support provides support in times of crisis, whether due to separation, divorce, loss, illness or other stressful events. The focus is on accompanying the family through difficult times.

Funds management:
- Help with household organization, budgeting, and other practical skills can be an important part of family assistance, especially when families face financial challenges.

Accompaniment to offices and institutions:
- Family assistance may also consist of accompanying family members to offices or institutions to ensure they have access to the necessary resources and services.

Networking:
- Family assistance promotes the formation of social networks and support systems, whether within the family, in the community or through access to other services and groups.

Cooperation with other services:
- Family support often involves working with other services and professionals to ensure that the family receives the best possible support. This may include working with schools, health services, childcare facilities, and other facilities.

Preventive measures:
- Family support can include preventive measures to promote the well-being of the family in the long term and prevent problems from developing.

Appreciative approach:
- An appreciative and respectful approach is a fundamental principle of family support. Professionals work together with family members to identify their strengths and achieve individual goals.

Family Assistance aims to support families in their diversity and taking into account their individual needs. It plays an important role in fostering resilience, stability and a positive environment for families.

Family Counseling

Family counseling is a professional service that aims to support families in different life situations, strengthen their relationships, overcome challenges, and promote positive change. Family counseling can be provided by professionals such as family therapists, psychologists, or social workers.

Goals of Family Counseling:
- The goals of family counseling can be varied, ranging from coping with communication problems, to helping them cope with crises, to promoting change in behaviors or dynamics in the family.

Crisis management:
- Family counseling is often in demand when families are facing crises such as separation, divorce, loss, serious illness, or other stressful events.

Communication Improvement:
- A common goal of family counseling is to improve communication within the family. This can include building understanding, empathy, and more effective communication skills.

Conflict resolution:
- Support in identifying and coping with conflicts within the family is a central component of family counselling. This includes the development of conflict resolution strategies and the promotion of a healthy culture of debate.

Change in behavior:
- Family counseling can be used to identify unhealthy behaviors within the family and promote positive change. This can be particularly relevant in the case of behavioral problems in children or adolescents.

Fostering cohesion and connection:
- Strengthening family ties and fostering cohesion are important aspects of family counselling. This can be especially relevant when family members are drifting apart or when the family is facing new challenges.

Parenting Skills:
- Family counseling can help parents improve their parenting skills by providing them with tools and resources to deal with the challenges of parenthood.

Strategies for blended families:
- In blended families involving children from different relationships, family counseling can help overcome the unique challenges of these structures and foster harmonious relationships.

Advice on life transitions:
- Family counseling can be supportive during important life transitions such as marriages, births, career changes, or adolescent transitions into adulthood.

Confidentiality and neutrality:
- Family counselors often act as neutral facilitators, providing a safe space for family members to talk openly about their challenges. Confidentiality is an important principle here.

Family counseling can take various forms, e.g. individual counseling, couples counseling or group counseling.

Family Therapy

Family therapy, also known as systemic therapy, is a form of psychotherapeutic intervention that aims to understand family relationships, manage conflicts, and promote positive changes in the family. The focus is on the consideration of the family as a social system in which the interactions and relationships between family members play a central role.

Systemic Approach:
- The systemic approach to family therapy views the family as a dynamic system in which each member is in relationship with the others. Changes in one area can have an impact on the entire system.

Goals of Family Therapy:
- The goals of family therapy can be manifold, ranging from improving communication and conflict resolution to managing crises, promoting understanding and support in change processes.

Identification of patterns and dynamics:
- An important aspect of family therapy is to identify the patterns and dynamics within the family that can contribute to problems. These can be recurring conflicts, communication patterns or unhealthy role distributions.

Communication Improvement:
- Family therapy often focuses on improving communication within the family. This includes learning effective communication skills, understanding different

communication styles, and identifying barriers in communication.

Conflict Resolution and Consensus Building:

- Family therapy helps families to resolve conflicts constructively and to reach consensus. This can be done by developing conflict resolution strategies and understanding different perspectives.

Strengthening relationships:

- There is also a focus on strengthening positive relationships within the family. This includes identifying and emphasizing strengths, as well as creating connections and support among family members.

Fostering empathy and understanding:

- Family therapy fosters empathy and understanding between family members. This can help break down prejudices and take into account the perspectives of each family member.

Resource orientation:

- Therapists in family therapy often work in a resource-oriented way, highlighting the family's existing strengths and resources to support positive change.

Inclusive approach:

- Family therapy can involve all family members, regardless of age or role. The inclusive approach makes it possible to take into account the diversity of perspectives and experiences within the family.

Flexibility and customization:

- Because families are different, family therapy requires flexibility and adaptation. Therapists adapt their methods and approaches to the specific needs and dynamics of each family.

Family therapy can take a variety of forms, including individual, couple, or group sessions. It provides a safe space where family members can talk openly about their problems and work together to find solutions.

Gender

Gender refers to the social, cultural, and psychological aspects of gender identity and gender roles that go beyond the biological differences between men and women. It is different from "sex", which is based on biological differences. Gender encompasses the expectations, roles, rights, and responsibilities that societies associate with the categories of "male" and "female."

Gender identity:
- Gender identity refers to one's personal inner experience and idea of one's gender, whether as male, female or otherwise. This identity may differ from the biological assignment.

Gender role:
- Gender role refers to the socially constructed expectations, behaviors, and activities that are considered appropriate for men and women in a given society. Gender roles vary culturally and historically.

Gender stereotypes:
- Gender stereotypes are fixed, often simplistic ideas about how men and women should be or what characteristics they should have. These stereotypes can limit individual freedom and lead to discrimination.

Gender equality:

- Gender equality refers to the process of ensuring equal rights, responsibilities and opportunities for women and men in all sectors of society. It strives for equal treatment and evaluation regardless of gender.

Gender-Conscious Education:

- Gender-conscious parenting involves fostering an education that respects gender diversity and encourages children to freely develop their interests, skills, and identity, regardless of gender expectations.

Sexuality and Gender:

- The relationship between sexuality and gender refers to how gender roles and identities interact with sexual orientations and expressions. It includes the acceptance and recognition of different sexual orientations.

Gender mainstreaming:

- Gender mainstreaming is an approach that aims to integrate gender aspects into all policies and decision-making processes in order to reduce gender inequalities.

Gender Studies:

- Gender studies refers to scientific research on gender-specific issues, including the analysis of gender roles, gender identity, gender inequalities, and the impact of gender on society.

Non-Binary and Gender Diversity:

- Non-binary refers to gender identities that are not exclusively male or female. The recognition and acceptance of gender diversity promotes the diversity and uniqueness of individual gender identities.

Gender fluidity:

- Gender fluidity describes the experience of changes in gender identity over time. People who identify as genderfluid may experience different gender identities at different times.

Addressing gender issues is crucial for creating inclusive, equitable and diverse societies. It requires a critical reflection on social norms and the promotion of equality regardless of gender.

General promotion of education in the family

The "General Promotion of Education in the Family" refers to measures and support aimed at strengthening parents in their educational task and promoting the positive development of children. This support can take place at different levels, both state and municipal.

Parent Education Programs:
These programs provide parents with information and training on various topics related to child-rearing, such as developmental stages, communication with children, conflict resolution, and positive discipline.

Family Counseling:
Professional counseling services are available to families to help them cope with challenges and conflicts. This can be done by trained therapists, psychologists, or social workers.

Early intervention:
Early childhood development programs provide support and resources for parents of young children. This can include information about the needs of infants and young children, as well as suggestions for games and activities that promote their development.

Financialsupport:
Government benefits, such as family allowances or tax breaks, can provide financial support to families and help them meet their children's needs.

Community Centres:
Facilities that provide a place for families to meet, share resources, and receive support from other parents. Educational events, workshops and activities for children can also be offered here.

Parent-Child Programs:
Programs that encourage interaction between parents and children to build a positive bond. This includes shared activities, games, and learning opportunities.

Information materials:
Providing easy-to-understand materials on relevant topics such as health, nutrition, safety and education to provide parents with important information.

Flexibility in the world of work:
Measures that make it easier for parents to reconcile work and family life, such as flexible working hours, working from home or parental leave.

Promoting family education is crucial for the well-being of children and the development of a stable society. Comprehensive parental support helps ensure that children can grow up in a loving and supportive environment.

Health Literacy

Health literacy refers to the individual's ability to understand, evaluate, and use health information and make informed decisions based on it. It's about how well people are able to understand and apply health information to promote their own health and interact with the healthcare system.

Understanding Health Information:
- Health literacy involves understanding basic health information, including medical terms, symptoms, diagnoses, and treatment plans.

Critical evaluation of information:
- An important skill of health literacy is to critically evaluate information. This includes assessing the reliability of sources, understanding the risks and benefits of interventions, and distinguishing evidence-based information from opinions.

Healthcare Decision-Making:
- Health literacy empowers people to make informed decisions about their health. This includes the ability to understand different treatment options, weigh risks and benefits, and make decisions in collaboration with healthcare providers.

Communication with Healthcare Providers:
- An important aspect of health literacy is the ability to communicate effectively with healthcare providers. This includes asking questions, understanding instructions, and actively participating in the decision-making process.

Promoting self-management:
- Health literacy empowers people to self-manage their health. This includes implementing healthy lifestyle habits, adhering to medication schedules, and self-directed care.

Navigating the healthcare system:
- The ability to navigate the complex healthcare system is a component of health literacy. This includes understanding insurance information, making appointments, and using healthcare services.

Health-promoting lifestyle habits:
- Health literacy helps promote health-promoting lifestyle habits, such as regular physical activity, a balanced diet, adequate sleep, and avoiding harmful substances.

Consideration of cultural differences:
- Health literacy should take into account cultural differences. It is crucial that health information is presented in a way that is understandable and acceptable to different cultural groups.

Promoting Community Resources:
- A health-literate individual is able to use existing community resources to promote their health. These include health courses, community centers, and prevention programs.

Lifelong learning:
- Health literacy is a lifelong process of learning and adapting. It should be continuously improved and updated to keep up with new health information and technologies.

Promoting health literacy is important to strengthen people's ownership of their health and to improve the efficiency and effectiveness of the health system.

Health promotion

Health promotion refers to actions and strategies to improve the health and well-being of individuals and communities. It is based on the idea that health is not only the absence of disease, but encompasses a holistic state of physical, mental and social well-being.

Promoting health awareness:
- Health promotion aims to raise awareness of the importance of health. The understanding of individual responsibility for one's own health is promoted.

Prevention of diseases:
- An important aspect of health promotion is the prevention of diseases. This includes measures such as vaccinations, early detection of diseases, lifestyle changes and health-promoting behaviours.

Promote healthy lifestyle habits:
- The promotion of healthy lifestyle habits is at the heart of health promotion. These include eating a balanced diet, regular physical activity, getting enough sleep, and avoiding harmful substances.

Strengthening health literacy:
- Health literacy refers to the ability to understand, evaluate, and make decisions based on health information. Health promotion aims to strengthen the health literacy of the population.

Creating health-promoting environments:
- A healthy environment in the workplace, schools, communities, and other areas of life is crucial. This may include the availability of healthy food, access to sports facilities, and stress-free working conditions.

Promote mental health:

- Promoting mental health is an important part of health promotion. Measures include reducing stigma, providing access to psychological support, and promoting stress management strategies.

Health promotion in the workplace:

- Workplace-based health promotion includes measures to create a healthy working environment, including ergonomic conditions, company sports programs and workplace mental health interventions.

Community-oriented approaches:

- Community-oriented health promotion actively involves the community in the planning and implementation of health interventions. This promotes personal responsibility and takes local needs into account.

Health promotion through education:

- Educational programs play a crucial role in health promotion. Information on health issues, prevention and healthy lifestyle habits is provided.

Intersectional approaches:

- Intersectional approaches take into account different dimensions such as gender, age, socioeconomic status, and ethnic background to ensure that health promotion is relevant to all populations.

Fostering partnerships:

- Health promotion is often done in collaboration with various actors, including government agencies, community organizations, educational institutions, and businesses.

Health promotion in the lifespan:

- Health promotion should take place throughout the lifespan, from early childhood to old age. This allows for a comprehensive approach to promoting health.

Health promotion emphasizes the proactive design of living conditions to improve health, prevent disease and increase quality of life. A holistic approach that takes into account individual responsibility, social determinants of health, and preventive measures helps to bring about sustainable positive changes for the health of a society.

Health Social Work

Health social work is a field of social work that focuses on the intersection between social and health aspects. It addresses the social determinants of health and provides support to people in health facilities and in the community.

Health promotion and prevention:
- Health social work is committed to promoting health and disease prevention. This may include the development and implementation of programs to promote healthy lifestyle habits and prevent disease.

Support in coping with the disease:
- Health social workers provide support for people facing health challenges. This may include coping with diagnoses, adapting to chronic illnesses, or processing trauma.

Psychosocial support:
- The provision of psychosocial support is a central aspect of health social work. This includes emotional support, counseling, and mental health promotion.

Patient and family counselling:
- Health social workers provide counseling services to patients and their families. This may include information on

disease management, resources, financial support, and decision-making.

Case Management:

- Health social workers are often involved in case management. They coordinate the various aspects of care, ensure that the patient's needs are met, and work with various healthcare professionals.

Transition from the clinic to the community:

- Health social work supports the transition from clinical care to community. This may include planning follow-up, ensuring support services, and promoting continuity of care.

Health promotion in communities:

- In community work, health social workers engage in projects and programs to promote health in the community. They work to influence social determinants of health and strengthen health literacy in the population.

Interdisciplinary cooperation:

- Health social workers work closely with other healthcare professionals, including doctors, nurses, therapists, and social service workers, to provide comprehensive care.

Ethics and Social Justice:

- Ethics and social justice are central principles in health social work. They advocate for fair and equitable health care for all and take ethical issues into account in the health context.

Research and Evaluation:

- Health social workers can participate in research and evaluation projects to review the effectiveness of interventions and promote best practices.

Health social work plays a crucial role in addressing the social determinants of health and ensuring that people not only have access to health care, but also receive support for their social and psychosocial needs.

Help Plan

A help plan is a written document that is created within the framework of child and youth welfare. It serves to record the individual needs, goals and measures for children, young people or families who need support due to special difficulties. The help plan process is a central element of educational aid.

Needs assessment and diagnosis:
- The help plan process begins with a comprehensive needs assessment and diagnosis. The individual challenges, needs and resources of the person or family concerned are analyzed.

Objectives and objectives:
- On the basis of the diagnosis, concrete goals are set. These goals are individually tailored to the needs of the person or family concerned and are intended to promote positive change.

Planning of measures:
- The assistance plan contains a detailed list of planned measures and interventions. These can be outpatient assistance, day-care or inpatient measures, school support, therapeutic interventions and other support services.

Participation of those affected:
- The aid plan process is designed to be participatory. Those affected, especially children and young people, are actively involved in the preparation of the help plan. Your opinions, needs and perspectives are incorporated into the planning.

Network and Cooperation:
- The help plan process involves various actors such as social workers, therapists, teachers, doctors and other professionals. Cooperation between stakeholders is

recorded in the aid plan to ensure effective and coordinated support.

Temporal perspective:

- The assistance plan includes a time perspective that specifies the period over which the measures are to be implemented. Periodic reviews and adjustments may be foreseen.

Evaluation and review:

- The aid plan provides for regular evaluation phases in which the progress of the measures is reviewed. In doing so, it is analysed whether the set goals have been achieved and whether adjustments are necessary.

Documentation:

- All steps in the help plan process are carefully documented. This includes the assessment of needs, goal setting, action planning, participation of those affected, networking, time perspective and evaluation results.

Data protection and confidentiality:

- The help plan takes into account the privacy and confidentiality of the information. Only relevant information is shared, and data subjects are informed who has access to the data.

Crisis management:

- The assistance plan may also include crisis management, which specifies how to act in acute emergency situations to ensure the safety and well-being of the affected person.

Assistance plans serve as a guideline for the planning and implementation of support measures in child and youth welfare. They promote transparency, cooperation between the actors involved and the alignment of measures with the individual needs of those affected.

Help Planning

Assistance planning is a structured procedure in child and youth welfare that serves to plan and implement individual help for children, young people and families. The assistance plan specifies which measures and assistance are necessary to achieve the individual needs and goals of those affected. Some aspects of aid planning include

Needs assessment and diagnostics:
- Aid planning begins with a careful assessment of needs and a diagnosis of the situation. In doing so, the individual strengths, resources, but also problems and challenges are recorded.

Objective:
- On the basis of the needs assessment, clear and realistic goals are set. These goals are intended to improve the living conditions of the people concerned and enable positive changes.

Participation of those affected:
- The aid planning provides for the active participation of the affected children, young people and families. Their opinions, wishes and concerns are taken into account in order to increase the acceptance and effectiveness of the measures.

Planning of measures:
- Concrete measures are developed on the basis of the objectives. These can be outpatient support services, therapeutic services, school measures, forms of housing or other forms of assistance.

Temporal perspective:
- Aid planning includes a temporal perspective. It specifies the period over which the planned measures are to be

carried out and when reviews and evaluations are to take place.

Professions and actors involved:

- Aid planning requires the cooperation of different professions and actors, such as social workers, teachers, therapists, doctors and other professionals. The tasks and responsibilities are clearly defined.

Evaluation phases:

- The aid planning provides for regular evaluation phases in which it is checked whether the set goals have been achieved. If necessary, adjustments can be made to respond to changing conditions.

Documentation:

- All steps of help planning are carefully documented. This includes the assessment of needs, goal setting, action planning, participation of those affected, time perspective, cooperation between stakeholders and evaluation results.

Data protection and confidentiality:

- Special attention is paid to data protection and confidentiality of information during assistance planning. Only relevant information will be shared, and data subjects will be informed about how their data will be handled.

Participation and empowerment:

- Aid planning promotes the participation of those affected and strives for empowerment. The aim is to strengthen the self-determination and co-responsibility of the persons concerned.

Aid planning is a dynamic process that adapts flexibly to changing needs and developments. It forms the basis for effective, needs-based support in child and youth welfare that is tailored to the individual situation.

Home help

Domestic help refers to support services provided in the household to help people cope with their daily tasks. These services may be necessary in various situations, such as illness, after surgery, during pregnancy, or other life circumstances that affect the ability to manage housekeeping.

Responsibilities of the domestic helper:
- Domestic helpers can assist with a variety of household tasks, including cleaning, laundry, shopping, meal preparation, caring for children or the elderly, and other household services.

Applications:
- Domestic help may be necessary in various life situations, including during recovery from illness or surgery, chronic illnesses, pregnancy and childbirth, old age, or other special circumstances.

Availability of domestic helpers:
- Domestic helpers can be professional service providers arranged by agencies, or informal caregivers, such as friends, family members, or neighbors, who offer support when needed.

Professional domestic helpers:
- Professional domestic helpers provided by agencies or service providers can be specially trained and provide targeted support in different areas, depending on the individual needs of the person.

Financing of domestic help:
- Funding for domestic help may vary by country, region and individual circumstances. In some cases, health insurance, long-term care insurance, or other social benefits can cover the cost of professional domestic help.

Independent organization:

- In some cases, people organise domestic help on their own. This may mean hiring a private individual directly or relying on volunteer help from their social circle.

Support for families:

- Domestic help can be an important support, especially for families with young children or people caring for elderly family members, to cope with everyday life.

Flexible services:

- Professional domestic helpers often offer flexible services tailored to the needs of the individual. This can include regular support or temporary help during special life situations.

Ethical considerations:

- When organizing domestic help, it is important to take into account ethical considerations regarding the privacy and needs of the person being cared for. Respectful communication and respect for personal dignity are paramount.

Societal benefits:

- Domestic help helps to improve the quality of life of people in different life situations. It makes it possible to cope with everyday life and supports independence, especially in the case of health restrictions.

The organization of domestic help depends heavily on individual needs, financial capabilities and available resources. In many countries, there are also local non-profit organizations that can help organize domestic help.

Home Nursing

Home nursing, also known as outpatient care or homecare, includes the medical and nursing care of patients in their own home. It offers an alternative to inpatient care and enables people to remain in their familiar surroundings despite illness or disability.

Health care:
- Home health care includes the provision of medical care by qualified nursing staff. This includes administering medications, treating wounds, monitoring vital signs, and performing medical procedures.

Care and support:
- Home health care nurses not only provide medical care, but also support with everyday activities such as bathing, dressing, eating, and mobility. They promote the independence of the patient as far as health permits.

Support for the chronically ill:
- Home health care is especially relevant for people with chronic conditions who require continuous care and monitoring. Caregivers can monitor health, monitor medication intake, and make adjustments as needed.

Rehabilitation:
- After hospitalization or surgery, home health care can be part of the rehabilitation process. Caregivers provide support with exercises, physiotherapy and regaining functionality.

Hospice and palliative care:
- For patients in advanced stages of a serious illness, home health care provides palliative care. The aim is to improve quality of life, alleviate symptoms and provide support for patients and their families.

Psycho-social support:
- In addition to physical care, caregivers also provide psychosocial support in the home environment. This may include providing emotional support for patients and their families to deal with the challenges of the disease.

Patient and family induction:
- Home health care nurses play an important role in educating patients and their families about health status, necessary care, and self-management strategies.

Coordination of care:
- Coordination of care is crucial, especially when multiple caregivers or therapists are involved in the care process. Home nursing coordinates the different aspects of care to ensure coherent care.

Provision of medical aids:
- Home nursing provides the necessary aids and medical equipment in the home environment. This may include wheelchairs, walkers, nursing beds, and other specialized equipment.

Continuous monitoring and reporting:
- Home health care nurses continuously monitor patients' health and report to doctors and other healthcare providers. This helps to make quick adjustments in the care plan.

Home care is often a valuable option for people who want to be cared for in their familiar environment. It supports independence, promotes recovery and improves the quality of life of patients, especially when inpatient care is not absolutely necessary.

Housekeeping help

Domestic help refers to household support services that aim to make everyday life easier and to help people cope with housekeeping tasks. This type of help can be particularly important for people with health restrictions, the elderly or people in special life situations.

Tasks of the housekeeping help:
- Housekeeping help includes a variety of household tasks, including cleaning, laundry, ironing, shopping, preparing meals, tidying up, and other household activities.

Target groups:
- The target groups for domestic help can be diverse and include the elderly, people with health restrictions, families with young children, people in the recovery phase after illness or surgery, as well as other people in special life situations.

Professional Service Providers:
- Housekeeping help can be provided by professional service providers, care agencies or domestic helpers. These service providers may have specially trained staff to meet the individual needs of clients.

Flexible Support:
- The type of support can be customized according to your needs and individual requirements. Some people need regular, daily help, while others may only need temporary support in certain life situations.

Financing of housekeeping assistance:
- Funding for housekeeping assistance can be provided through a variety of sources, including private payments, long-term care insurance, public health insurance, or other social support services, which may vary by country.

Adaptation to individual needs:
- Professional housekeeping assistants often adapt their services to the individual needs of the clients. This may mean prioritizing certain tasks or helping at different intervals.

Combination with care services:
- In some cases, domestic help is offered in conjunction with care services to provide comprehensive support for people with more complex needs.

Support for relatives:
- Housekeeping help can also help reduce the burden on family members who may not be able to handle all household tasks.

Promoting self-reliance:
- One of the goals of housekeeping help is to promote the independence of clients by enabling them to live in their own homes for as long as possible and to manage their daily activities independently.

Communication and arrangements:
- Successful housekeeping help requires clear communication between the service providers and the clients. This includes setting tasks, schedules, individual preferences and all other relevant aspects.

Domestic care plays an important role in helping people maintain an orderly and comfortable household, especially when health or personal circumstances require help.

Inclusion

Inclusion is a comprehensive approach to promoting the full participation and equality of all people in society, regardless of individual differences and characteristics. The concept of inclusion extends to various areas of life such as education, work, leisure and social integration.

Definition of inclusion:
- Inclusion refers to the comprehensive process that aims to break down barriers and enable all people to fully participate and participate in all areas of society, regardless of gender, age, ethnic origin, disability or other characteristics.

Inclusive Education:
- In inclusive education, the aim is to ensure that all pupils, regardless of their individual requirements and needs, are taught together in regular schools. This includes measures such as barrier-free school buildings, individualised teaching and support from specialised specialists.

Workplace inclusion:
- Inclusion in the workplace means that people with different skills and backgrounds have the same professional opportunities and rights. Employers are implementing inclusive practices to promote the diversity of their workforce and create an accessible workplace.

Accessibility:
- Accessibility is a fundamental principle of inclusion. This includes physical accessibility, but also the provision of information in different formats to ensure that people with different abilities and needs can participate equally.

Social inclusion:
- Social inclusion aims to break down social barriers and foster a sense of belonging for all members of society. This

can be achieved through social programs, cultural activities, and community projects.

Participation and co-determination:

- Inclusion does not only mean physical presence, but also active participation and co-determination. All people should have the opportunity to express their opinions, help shape decisions and actively participate in social life.

Recognition of diversity:

- Inclusion respects and values the diversity of people. This includes cultural, ethnic, linguistic, religious, and other differences. The appreciation of diversity helps to break down prejudices and promote tolerant and respectful coexistence.

Empowerment:

- Inclusion promotes empowerment by encouraging people to develop their potential, experience self-determination, and use their individual strengths.

Social awareness:

- Inclusion requires raising awareness in society of the needs and rights of all people. This can be promoted through awareness campaigns, training and dialogues.

Legal basis:

- In many countries, laws and regulations have been implemented to protect the rights of people with different needs and to ensure their inclusive participation in different areas of life.

Promoting inclusion helps to create a society where diversity is seen as an enrichment and where all people can enjoy equal opportunities and rights. It is a continuous process that requires joint efforts by individuals, institutions and society as a whole.

Inclusiveness

Inclusivity refers to the principle and practice of equal inclusion and participation of people in all walks of life, regardless of their individual differences and backgrounds. It's about creating an environment that values diversity, breaks down barriers, and ensures that all members of the community have equal opportunities and rights.

Respecting diversity:
- Inclusivity starts with respecting and acknowledging the diversity of people. This includes differences in gender, age, ethnicity, religion, sexual orientation, disabilities, and other characteristics.

Promoting equality:
- Inclusivity strives for equality for all members of society. This includes equal opportunities in education, the workplace, leisure and all other areas of life.

Ensuring accessibility:
- Inclusivity requires the removal of barriers, both physical and social. This includes barrier-free access to buildings, barrier-free communication, and creating an environment that is accessible to all.

Enabling participation:
- Inclusivity aims to enable the active participation of all people. This means not only presence, but also inclusion in decision-making processes, activities, and social interactions.

Cultural Sensitivity:
- An inclusive environment requires cultural sensitivity and respect for different cultural backgrounds. This helps to value cultural diversity and break down prejudices.

Education and Awareness:
- Inclusivity is promoted through education and awareness. This includes diversity education, awareness training, and fostering knowledge about the needs and perspectives of different groups.

Empathy and understanding:
- Inclusivity requires empathy and understanding of other people's life situations. This helps break down prejudice and create a supportive community.

Community orientation:
- Inclusivity fosters a community orientation in which the needs of the individual are aligned with the needs of the community. This creates a sense of belonging and cohesion.

Social Responsibility:
- Inclusivity emphasizes the social responsibility of each individual and organization to create an environment that is conducive to all members of society.

Legal framework:
- Many countries have legal frameworks in place to protect people's rights and promote inclusivity. These laws serve as the basis for protecting against discrimination and ensuring equality.

Inclusivity is not only a goal, but also an ongoing process that requires a constant effort to change and improve. It is an attitude and a practice that aims to create a more just and inclusive society.

Integration

Integration refers to the process of integrating people from different cultural, social, or ethnic backgrounds into existing communities or structures. The aim is to promote the active participation and coexistence of different groups, while respecting diversity and individual identities.

Social integration:
- Social integration refers to the integration of people into existing social structures. This may include participating in joint activities, socializing, and gaining acceptance in social groups.

Educational integration:
- Educational integration means that pupils from different backgrounds are taught together in mainstream schools. The aim is to ensure equal opportunities in the field of education.

Labour market integration:
- Labour market integration refers to integrating people from different backgrounds into the labour market. This includes equal employment opportunities, fair pay and a non-discriminatory working environment.

Cultural Integration:
- Cultural integration means that people can maintain their own cultural identity while living in a wider cultural community. It is about the exchange and mutual recognition of different forms of cultural expression.

Linguistic integration:
- Linguistic integration refers to people being able to learn and use the language of the country in which they live. Language plays a crucial role in participation in social life.

Equal rights and equal opportunities:

- Integration strives for equal rights and equal opportunities for all members of society. This includes access to education, jobs, health care, and other resources.

Social values and norms:

- Integration takes into account social values and norms and promotes an understanding of them. At the same time, individual values and norms should be respected.

Mutual acceptance:

- Integration promotes mutual acceptance and tolerance between different groups. This helps to break down prejudices and enable harmonious coexistence.

Community life:

- Integration aims to create a sense of community in which people can actively participate in social life, regardless of their origin.

Legal framework:

- Many countries have enacted laws and regulations to protect the rights of migrants and other groups and to promote their integration.

Integration is a dynamic process that involves the adaptation of the host society and the individual groups. A successful integration model takes into account the needs of all stakeholders and strives for a common, inclusive society.

Integration assistance for people with disabilities

Integration assistance for people with disabilities refers to various measures and support services aimed at enabling people with disabilities to participate in social life on an equal footing. In many countries, there are special legal regulations and programmes that organise integration assistance.

Definition of disability:
- The definition of disability may vary by country and legislation. Integration assistance is usually aimed at people who are dependent on support due to physical, mental or emotional impairments.

Legal basis:
- In many countries, there are special laws or regulations that regulate integration assistance for people with disabilities. These laws are designed to ensure that people with disabilities receive the necessary support to actively participate in social life.

Individual clarification of needs:
- Integration assistance is often based on an individual assessment of needs. This means that the support is tailored to the individual needs and abilities of the person with a disability.

Areas of support:
- Integration assistance can cover various areas, including education, work, housing, mobility, social integration and leisure activities.

Assistance services:
- Assistance services can be part of integration assistance. This includes personal assistance in everyday life, assistance

with mobility, support with communication and other supportive measures.

Accessibility:

- The creation of accessibility is an important aspect of integration assistance. This refers to physical accessibility in buildings and public transport, as well as the accessibility of information and communication.

Participation in working life:

- Integration assistance is often aimed at facilitating access to the labour market for people with disabilities. This can be done through vocational rehabilitation, on-the-job support, or special job offers.

Housing:

- Integration assistance can also include housing services that enable people with disabilities to live independently.

Early intervention:

- In some cases, integration assistance also includes early intervention for children with disabilities in order to support their development in the best possible way.

Cooperation with various actors:

- Integration assistance often requires the cooperation of different actors, including social services, educational institutions, employers, disability organisations and others.

The aim of integration assistance is to enable people with disabilities to lead as self-determined a life as possible and to participate fully in social life.

Integration Service

An Integration Service (IFD) is an institution that supports people with disabilities in their integration into the labour market. These services exist in many countries and work closely with various stakeholders, including people with disabilities, employers, rehabilitation providers and other disability services.

Target group:
- The Integration Service is aimed at people with disabilities who need special support in their professional integration due to their health restrictions.

Individual advice and support:
- IFDs offer individualized counseling and support to address the specific needs and abilities of people with disabilities. This may include identifying suitable job opportunities and developing integration strategies.

Cooperation with employers:
- IFDs work closely with employers to find suitable jobs for people with disabilities. This can include raising awareness among employers of the potential of people with disabilities.

Workplace analyses:
- IFDs conduct workplace analyses to ensure that the workplace meets the needs and abilities of people with disabilities. They can also make recommendations for necessary adjustments or support services.

Mediation and accompaniment:
- The Integration Service supports the placement of suitable jobs and accompanies people with disabilities during the integration process. This may include on-the-job training.

Networking:

- IFDs work in a network of different actors, including rehabilitation providers, employment agencies, social welfare offices and other organisations. The cooperation enables comprehensive support for people with disabilities.

Promoting Diversity and Inclusion:

- IFDs promote diversity and inclusion in the workplace. They are committed to ensuring that people with different types of disabilities have equal access to employment opportunities.

Qualification and training:

- IFDs often provide skills and training to strengthen the professional skills and independence of people with disabilities.

Support in working life:

- The integration service can also provide support during the employment relationship in order to ensure sustainable integration. This may include, for example, adapting working conditions or arranging support services.

Implementation of legal framework:

- IFDs take into account the applicable legal framework for the professional integration of people with disabilities. This may include national laws and regulations, as well as international conventions.

The work of the integration services is aimed at promoting equal opportunities for people with disabilities in the labour market and enabling them to participate fully in working life.

Intercultural Competence

Intercultural competence refers to the ability to act effectively and respectfully in intercultural situations. This competency includes the understanding of cultural differences, the ability to communicate and collaborate in an intercultural environment, and the willingness to engage with different cultural perspectives.

Cultural Awareness:
- Intercultural competence starts with a strong cultural awareness. It includes understanding one's own cultural backgrounds as well as acknowledging and appreciating the diversity of other cultures.

Intercultural sensitivity:
- Sensitivity to cultural differences is crucial. This includes recognizing differences in behaviors, values, communication styles, and thought patterns.

Communication skills:
- Effective communication in an intercultural context requires the ability to express oneself clearly and listen. This also includes taking cultural differences into account in non-verbal communication.

Empathy:
- Empathy, empathizing with the perspectives of others, is a central component of intercultural competence. This allows for a deeper understanding of the feelings and perspectives of people from other cultures.

Flexibility and adaptability:
- Intercultural competence requires flexibility and the ability to adapt to different social norms and behaviors. This is especially true when it comes to business practices, work ethics, and interpersonal relationships.

Conflict Resolution Skills:

- Conflicts can arise due to cultural differences. Intercultural competence includes the ability to resolve conflicts effectively, taking into account different cultural contexts.

Self-reflection:

- The willingness to self-reflect is important in order to recognize one's own cultural imprints and prejudices. This allows for an open attitude towards new perspectives.

Tolerance and openness:

- A tolerant and open attitude towards different lifestyles, values and beliefs is an essential part of intercultural competence.

Willingness to learn:

- Intercultural competence includes a continuous willingness to learn. This means constantly learning and opening up to new cultural experiences.

Intercultural trainings:

- Participation in intercultural trainings can help to develop specific skills and knowledge to operate successfully in intercultural contexts.

Professional Application:

- In professional application, cross-cultural competence means having the ability to work effectively with international teams, understanding global business practices, and taking into account cultural differences in customer care.

Intercultural competence is crucial in a globalized world where people from different cultures interact on a personal and professional level. Developing this competency helps to avoid misunderstandings, strengthen interpersonal relationships, and foster success in an increasingly interconnected society.

Intercultural openness

Cross-cultural openness refers to the process by which organizations, institutions, or communities shape their structures, practices, and ways of thinking in such a way that they actively recognize, respect, and promote cultural diversity and differences. The aim is to create an inclusive environment in which people from different cultural backgrounds can participate on an equal footing and develop their individual potential.

Recognition of diversity:
- Intercultural openness begins with the conscious recognition and appreciation of diversity in a community or organization. This includes cultural, ethnic, religious, linguistic and other differences.

Inclusive structures and policies:
- Organizations that open up interculturally adapt their structures and policies to promote inclusion and equal opportunities. This may include developing policies to prevent discrimination and promote diversity.

Creating Awareness:
- Intercultural openness involves fostering an awareness of cultural differences and the impact of stereotypes and prejudices. Training and awareness-raising activities can help to promote this awareness.

Participation and co-determination:
- People from different cultural backgrounds should be involved in decision-making processes. Intercultural openness promotes the participation and co-determination of all members of the community or organization.

Accessibility:
- Intercultural openness also includes the creation of barrier-free access for all members, regardless of their cultural

background. This can include physical accessibility, but also access to information and services.

Intercultural Communication:

- Effective communication across cultural boundaries is an essential part of intercultural openness. This includes the promotion of multilingual communication strategies and the consideration of cultural differences in communication.

Education and training:

- Organizations can provide cross-cultural training and education to promote understanding of cultural diversity and prepare employees for cross-cultural interactions.

Resources for Migrants and Minorities:

- Intercultural openness involves providing resources and support services tailored to the needs of migrants, ethnic minorities or other cultural groups.

Promotion of cultural events:

- Hosting and supporting cultural events and activities helps promote diversity and create an inclusive environment.

Evaluation and adaptation:

- Regular evaluations help to measure progress in terms of intercultural openness. Based on the results, adjustments can be made to the measures to increase effectiveness.

Intercultural openness is a continuous process that requires extensive commitment and constant adaptation. Successful implementation can lead to better integration, a positive working and living environment, and a more respectful interaction.

Interculturality

Interculturality refers to the coexistence and interaction of people from different cultural backgrounds. The term emphasizes mutual influence, dialogue and understanding between different cultures.

Cultural diversity:
- Interculturality is based on the recognition and appreciation of cultural diversity. She does not see cultural differences as obstacles, but as an enrichment.

Reciprocal relationships:
- The intercultural approach emphasizes reciprocal relationships and exchange between different cultures. It's about learning from each other and growing together.

Respect and tolerance:
- Interculturality is based on respect and tolerance towards other cultures. It requires an understanding of different values, norms and ways of life.

Cultural Dialogue:
- At the heart of interculturality is cultural dialogue, in which people from different cultural backgrounds actively communicate and exchange ideas with each other. This fosters mutual understanding.

Integration and inclusion:
- Interculturality strives for the integration and inclusion of people from different cultural backgrounds in all areas of society, be it education, work or leisure.

Community Building:
- Interculturality promotes the formation of community structures in which people from different backgrounds can live together and cooperate.

Cultural Criticism:
- The intercultural approach can also include cultural criticism by pointing out and opposing existing prejudices, stereotypes and discrimination.

Bilingualism and multilingualism:
- Interculturality is often considered in the context of bilingualism and multilingualism, as it promotes the use and cultivation of different languages.

Global Perspective:
- Interculturality takes a global perspective and takes into account the complex relationships between different cultures on an international level.

Intercultural Competence:
- The acquisition of intercultural competence, i.e. the ability to act effectively in intercultural situations, is considered an important aspect. This includes intercultural sensitivity, communication skills, and conflict resolution skills.

Promoting diversity:
- Interculturality fosters diversity and creates environments where different cultural perspectives are seen as a strength.

Interculturality is an approach to promoting peace, understanding and cooperation between people from different cultural backgrounds. It plays an important role in an increasingly globalized world where intercultural skills are of great importance.

Interdisciplinarity

Interdisciplinarity refers to the collaboration and exchange between different disciplines or disciplines to understand, explore, and solve complex problems. The approach of interdisciplinarity goes beyond the boundaries of individual disciplines and promotes a holistic view.

Collaboration between different disciplines:
- Interdisciplinarity involves the collaboration of experts from different disciplines. These can be, for example, natural scientists, social scientists, technologists and artists.

Holistic perspective:
- The interdisciplinary approach strives for a holistic perspective that takes into account different aspects of a topic or problem. The aim is to develop more comprehensive solutions.

Overlaps of knowledge and methods:
- Interdisciplinary teams bring together different types of knowledge, methods and ways of thinking. This creates synergies and new insights, which are made possible by the cooperation of the disciplines.

Solving complex problems:
- The interdisciplinary approach is often chosen to address complex problems that cannot be solved by a single discipline alone. Bringing together expertise helps to find more comprehensive solutions.

Creativity and innovation:
- By sharing ideas and perspectives from different disciplines, creativity can be fostered and innovation stimulated. New approaches and solutions can emerge.

Communication and understanding:
- Interdisciplinary teams require clear communication and an understanding of the terminology and methods of other disciplines. This contributes to effective collaboration.

Research projects and studies:
- In research, interdisciplinary projects are common, as they can contribute to gaining deeper insights into complex phenomena. This can be the case in fields such as environmental science, medicine, technology, and social sciences.

Flexibility and openness:
- Interdisciplinarity requires flexibility and openness to new ideas and approaches. It's about going beyond traditional thought patterns and integrating different perspectives.

Education and apprenticeship:
- Higher education is increasingly adopting interdisciplinary teaching approaches to prepare students for a broader perspective and strengthen their collaborative skills.

Tackling societal challenges:
- Interdisciplinary approaches are often necessary to address complex societal challenges that affect a variety of disciplines, such as health, climate change, and social injustice.

Interdisciplinarity helps to harness the diversity of perspectives and develop more comprehensive solutions to complex challenges in different fields.

Intervention

Intervention refers to targeted actions or interventions taken to influence, improve, or change a situation. Interventions can take place in a variety of contexts, including medical, social, psychological, and educational fields. Some key aspects of the intervention include:

Targeted measures:
- Interventions are targeted and focused on a specific outcome or goal. They are designed to bring about positive change or solve a problem.

Market analysis:
- Before an intervention is carried out, a needs assessment is often carried out to identify the exact need or problem that the intervention is targeting.

Early intervention:
- In some cases, interventions are used early to prevent problems from developing or to counteract them early before they become more severe.

Individualized approaches:
- Interventions can be tailored to individual needs, especially in the areas of health, education and social work. This allows for targeted support.

Crisis intervention:
- Crisis intervention refers to actions taken to help people in acute emergencies or crisis situations. This may include emotional support, resource allocation, or other forms of help.

Socio-pedagogical intervention:
- In the pedagogical field, interventions can be used to promote the learning and social development of pupils.

131

This can be done, for example, through targeted support measures.

Behavioral Intervention:

- Interventions in the field of behavioral psychology are used to change or modify behaviors. This can be relevant in both clinical and educational contexts.

Health Intervention:

- Health interventions include actions to promote health, prevent disease, or help manage health problems.

Evaluation and monitoring:

- Interventions are often evaluated to verify their effectiveness. This includes regularly monitoring and adjusting measures to ensure they have the intended effect.

Participation of those affected:

- Many interventions try to actively involve those affected and to include their perspectives and needs in the planning and implementation process.

Multidisciplinary approach:

- Complex problems often require a multidisciplinary approach, with professionals from different fields working together to develop more comprehensive solutions.

Continuity and long-term effects:

- Some interventions aim at long-term change and require continuous support over a longer period of time to achieve sustainable impact.

Interventions can take place at different levels, from individual interventions to community or even societal actions. The success of an intervention often depends on careful planning, implementation and evaluation.

Interviewing techniques

Interviewing techniques are skills and strategies that are used to communicate effectively with others, share opinions, share information, and build relationships. Successful interviewing can be important in different contexts, be it professional, personal, or therapeutic. The following are some important conversational techniques:

Active listening:
- Active listening is a central technique in which the interlocutor is attentive, asks questions, gives summaries, and responds empathetically to what the other person is saying. This promotes understanding and shows interest.

Ask open-ended questions:
- Open-ended questions encourage detailed answers and encourage the opening of the conversation. They often start with "what", "why" or "how" and give the interlocutor space to express their thoughts.

Ask closed-ended questions:
- Closed-ended questions usually require short, concise answers such as "yes" or "no." They are used to clarify specific information or to steer the conversation.

Paraphrase:
- Paraphrasing means repeating in one's own words what the interlocutor has said. This not only shows that you are paying attention, but also allows misunderstandings to be clarified.

Reflect:
- Reflecting refers to mirroring the emotions or feelings of the interlocutor. This fosters empathy and shows that you can put yourself in the other person's shoes.
-

Using I-Messages:
- Instead of assigning blame, I-messages can be used to communicate one's own feelings and needs. For example, "I feel frustrated when..."

Pay attention to non-verbal communication:
- Non-verbal signals such as body language, facial expressions, gestures and tone of voice play a crucial role in conversation. Consciously understanding and controlling these signals can improve communication.

Give feedback:
- Constructive feedback makes it possible to reinforce positive behaviors and address areas for improvement. It should be specific, factual and respectful.

Conversational control:
- The ability to steer the conversation and focus on the main topic is important. This prevents the conversation from going off topic.

Use breaks:
- Pauses can be used to give the interlocutor time to think about an answer themselves. They help to avoid being overwhelmed.

Showing empathy:
- Empathy means being able to understand and empathize with the other person's perspective. It creates a supportive conversational atmosphere.

Solution-oriented interviewing:
- Solution-oriented interviewing focuses on finding constructive solutions rather than focusing on problems. This can be helpful in professional and personal contexts.

Gather feedback:
- During the conversation, it can be helpful to gather feedback to ensure that both parties are on the same page and avoid misunderstandings.

Setting boundaries:
- In some conversational situations, it's important to set clear boundaries and clearly communicate what's acceptable and what's not.

The effective application of these conversational techniques can lead to improved interpersonal relationships, more successful conflict management, and overall clear and positive communication.

Justice

Justice is a comprehensive concept based on fairness, equality, law, and moral principles. It refers to the fair distribution of resources, opportunities and rights in a society. Justice can be considered at various levels, including individual, social, economic, and legal justice.

Legal Justice:
- Legal justice refers to the fair application of laws and equal treatment before the law. This includes protecting the rights and freedoms of all citizens regardless of gender, race, religion or social status.

Social Justice:
- Social justice refers to the fair distribution of social resources, opportunities and burdens. It aims to reduce inequalities and ensure that all members of society have access to basic needs.

Economic Justice:
- Economic justice refers to the fair distribution of economic resources and opportunities. This includes access to education, jobs, decent pay and social safety nets.

Equity in Education:
- Equity in education refers to ensuring that everyone has access to quality education, regardless of social background or financial resources. This promotes equal opportunities for personal and professional development.

Environmental Justice:
- Environmental justice refers to the equitable distribution of environmental impacts and resources, regardless of social, economic, or ethical differences. This protects communities from environmental pressures.

International Justice:
- International justice refers to fair relations and interactions between nations. This includes issues such as trade, development aid, human rights and peace.

Restorative Justice:
- Restorative justice is an approach that focuses on restoring damage and relationships, rather than punishment. It emphasizes accountability, repairing damage and reintegrating perpetrators.

Equality and equality:
- Equality and equality are core principles of justice that ensure that people are treated equally regardless of gender, race, religion or other characteristics.

Equity in Healthcare:
- Health care equity refers to ensuring that all people have access to adequate health care, regardless of financial means or social status.

Participation and inclusion:
- Equity also involves the active participation of all members of a society in decision-making processes and the

promotion of inclusion to ensure that different voices are heard.

Justice is a fundamental principle that promotes social peace, protects fundamental rights and enables a balanced and inclusive society. It requires constant reflection on existing inequalities and efforts to address and minimize them.

Lifeworld orientation

Lifeworld orientation is a concept in social work that aims to place people's living environment at the center of professional practice. The aim is to understand the individual circumstances, experiences and needs of the clients and to include them in the support process.

Centering on the living environment:
- Lifeworld orientation focuses on people's living environment. This includes social relationships, the environment, cultural backgrounds, experiences and individual resources.

Holistic approach:
- The life-world orientation takes a holistic view of people. It is not only looked at certain problems or deficits, but also at strengths, resources and potential.

Participation of clients:
- A central aspect is the active participation of clients in the support process. Your perspectives and opinions are taken seriously, and solutions are worked out together.

Individual needs-orientation:
- The help and support is based on the individual needs of the clients. It's about finding tailor-made solutions that meet the specific circumstances of life.

Relationship orientation:
- The quality of the relationship between professional and client is a central component. Empathy, understanding and a respectful attitude promote positive cooperation.

Resource orientation:
- Lifeworld orientation focuses on the available resources of the clients. The goal is to empower and use these resources to create positive change.

Contextual interventions:
- Interventions are tailored to the specific social and cultural context of the clients. It takes into account how life circumstances and structures influence individual support needs.

Empowerment:
- Lifeworld orientation strives to strengthen the self-determination and ability of the clients to act. It's about giving them the tools to make decisions on their own responsibility and shape their lives.

Critical Reflection:
- Professionals in life-world orientation critically reflect on their own values and assumptions. This is important to avoid prejudice and promote an appreciative attitude towards diversity.

Continuity and long-termism:
- Support is not seen as a short-term measure, but as a long-term process. Continuity and long-term thinking contribute to bringing about lasting changes in the life situation of the clients.

Interdisciplinary cooperation:
- Life-world orientation promotes cooperation between different disciplines. By sharing perspectives and expertise, more comprehensive solutions can be developed.

Social Justice:
- The concept of lifeworld orientation also includes the commitment to social justice. It is about recognizing structural injustices and advocating for change at the individual and societal level.

Life-world orientation is particularly relevant in social fields of work such as youth welfare, social counselling, assistance for the disabled and care for the elderly. It contributes to making the practice of social work more person-centered and effective.

Mediation

Mediation is a structured process for the constructive resolution of conflicts by a neutral third party, the mediator. The aim of mediation is to support the parties to the conflict in finding a joint solution on their own responsibility and in a self-determined manner.

Neutral mediation:
- The mediator is neutral and impartial. He does not take a position on the conflict and has no decision-making power. Its role is to facilitate the communication process and support the parties in finding a solution on their own.

139

Voluntariness:
- Participation in mediation is voluntary. All parties involved must agree to the mediation process and show a willingness to actively participate in conflict resolution.

Confidentiality:
- A central principle of mediation is confidentiality. Everything that is discussed during the mediation remains confidential. This creates an open atmosphere of communication and encourages parties to express their concerns freely.

Ownership:
- The responsibility for resolving the conflict lies with the parties to the conflict themselves. The mediator supports them in developing their own solutions instead of imposing ready-made solutions on them.

Structured procedure:
- Mediation follows a structured process that typically involves different phases. This includes clarifying the issues of conflict, gathering information, identifying interests and needs, finding options, and agreeing on a solution.

Promotion of communication:
- The mediator encourages open and respectful communication between the parties. It helps to clarify misunderstandings and to address conflicts constructively.

Interest orientation:
- Instead of focusing on positions, mediation emphasizes the identification of interests and needs. The solutions should meet the interests of both parties.

Win-win solutions:
- The goal of mediation is to achieve win-win solutions where both parties benefit from the agreement. This is in contrast to a "zero-sum game" mentality, where one party wins means the other loses.

Flexibility:
- Mediation is flexible and can be adapted to the specific needs and dynamics of the conflict. The mediator can use various methods and techniques to make the process effective.

Long-Term Relationship Retention:
- Mediation aims to maintain or restore long-term relationships. This is especially important in contexts where the parties need to interact with each other even after the conflict has been resolved, such as in family or business relationships.

Mediation is used in a variety of contexts, such as family conflicts, divorces, neighborhood disputes, labor disputes, and trade disputes. The mediation process offers the parties to the conflict the opportunity to actively participate in the development of solutions, thus promoting ownership and cooperation.

Medical rehabilitation services

Medical rehabilitation services include a wide range of measures to improve or restore the health and participation of people with health impairments. These services aim to promote individual abilities, reduce functional limitations and support independence in everyday life.

Indication and prescription:
- Medical rehabilitation is usually prescribed by doctors when there is a medical need. This can be the case with various health conditions, including accidents, surgeries, chronic conditions, neurological disorders, or orthopedic problems.

Rehabilitation Goals:

- The goals of medical rehabilitation vary depending on individual needs. They can include improving mobility, reducing pain, restoring physical functions, promoting independence in everyday life or vocational rehabilitation.

Multidisciplinary teams:

- Rehabilitation is often carried out by multidisciplinary teams made up of various professionals such as physiotherapists, occupational therapists, speech therapists, psychologists and other specialists. This enables a holistic view of individual needs.

Physiotherapy:

- Physical therapy is an important component of medical rehabilitation. It includes exercises, manual techniques, and other physical interventions to improve physical function, reduce pain, and promote mobility.

Occupational therapy:

- Occupational therapy focuses on helping people perform everyday activities independently. This may include adapting environments, using assistive devices, and developing skills.

Speech therapy:

- Speech therapy is important if there are speech or swallowing disorders. Therapy may include improving communication skills and restoring swallowing function.

Psychological support:

- Psychological support is often part of rehabilitation, especially when psychosocial aspects affect recovery. This may include coping with stress, anxiety, or depression.

Vocational rehabilitation:

- Vocational rehabilitation aims to reintegrate people into professional life. This may include professional training, reskilling, job coaching, and other measures.

Outpatient and inpatient rehabilitation:
- Rehabilitation can be both outpatient and inpatient, depending on the severity of the impairment and the individual needs of the patient.

Prevention and aftercare:
- An important aspect of medical rehabilitation is also the prevention of further health problems as well as the provision of long-term follow-up care.

Payment:
- In many countries, the costs of medical rehabilitation are covered by health insurance, pension insurance or other social insurance. However, the exact regulation varies depending on the country and insurance system.

Medical rehabilitation plays a crucial role in helping people cope with health impairments and restore their quality of life.

Methods of Social Work

Social work methods are strategic approaches used by social workers to work with individuals, groups and communities and to address social problems. These methods can vary depending on the needs of the clients, the context and the goals of the intervention.

Case Diagnosis and Assessment:
- This is the process of systematically assessing individual, family, or community needs, resources, and challenges. It serves as a basis for the planning and implementation of interventions.

Case Management:
- Case management involves coordinating services and resources to meet clients' needs. It includes developing service plans, monitoring progress, and adjusting interventions as needed.

Counseling and Talk Therapy:
- This method aims to support people through conversations and help them overcome challenges, make decisions, and achieve their personal goals.

Group work:
- Group work refers to working with groups of people, whether in the form of therapeutic groups, support groups, or community-based groups. This method promotes the exchange of experiences and the development of supportive social networks.

Community work:
- This method focuses on working with communities to identify their strengths, mobilize resources, and collaboratively develop solutions to social problems.

Social Pedagogy:
- Social pedagogy combines pedagogical approaches with social work methods. It aims to promote the development of individuals and groups through education and support.

Social Policy Analysis:
- Social workers analyse and evaluate social policies to promote change at the policy level and ensure that clients' needs are adequately addressed.

Family work:
- This method focuses on working with families to solve relationship problems, support child-rearing, and improve the overall functioning of the family.

Community Organizing:
- Community organizing involves mobilizing communities to work together for social justice and positive change. This

may include organizing activities, protests, or political advocacy.

Mediation and Conflict Resolution:
- Social workers can act as mediators to resolve conflicts within families, groups, or communities and promote positive communication.

Participatory Research:
- Participatory research actively involves clients in the research process in order to understand their perspectives and experiences and in this way design relevant interventions.

Social workers often use a combination of these methods in their work to meet the diverse needs of their clients.

Migration

Migration refers to the migration of people from one place to another, either within a country or across national borders. People migrate for a variety of reasons, including economic opportunity, education, displacement from conflict or persecution, and social or cultural reasons.

Types of migration:
- There are different types of migration, including internal migration (within a country), international migration (between countries), labour migration, displacement and asylum seekers, return migration, and voluntary or forced migration.

Causes of migration:

- People migrate for a variety of reasons, including economic opportunity, better living conditions, education, political insecurity, persecution, natural disasters, and climatic changes.

Refugees and asylum seekers:

- Refugees are people fleeing persecution, conflict or serious human rights violations. Asylum seekers are people who seek protection in another country and apply for asylum in order to be recognised as refugees.

Integration and acculturation:

- Integration refers to the process by which migrants are integrated into the society of their host country. Acculturation describes the process of cultural adaptation that migrants experience as they adapt to the values, norms, and practices of the new culture.

Challenges of migration:

- Migrants may encounter various challenges, including cultural differences, language barriers, discrimination, lack of social support, and possible legal obstacles.

Brain Drain and Brain Gain:

- "Brain drain" refers to the brain drain from a country, while "brain gain" refers to the benefit a country derives from hosting highly skilled migrants.

Remittances:

- Many migrants send money back to their countries of origin, known as remittances. These funds can make an important contribution to economic development in the countries of origin.

Migration policy:

- Countries are developing migration policies to regulate the influx, stay, and integration of migrants. These policies can be restrictive or integration-oriented, and often depend on political, economic and social conditions.

Multiculturalism:

- Multiculturalism refers to the recognition and promotion of different cultures within a society. This approach aims to promote the integration of migrants, while at the same time valuing their cultural diversity.

Environmental triggers for migration:

- Climate change and environmental changes can lead to environmental migration when people leave their homes due to natural disasters, droughts or other environmental triggers.

  Migration is a complex and multifaceted phenomenon that has a significant impact on the countries of origin and destination, as well as on the migrants themselves. The discussion on migration encompasses social, economic, political and cultural aspects.

Migration Counselling

Migration counseling refers to counseling services that help people with their migration plans and processes. These counselling services can cover a wide range of topics, ranging from legal aspects to social integration steps.

Legal advice:

- Migration consultants often offer legal advice regarding immigration rules and regulations. This may include clarifying visa options, immigration applications, asylum procedures, and other legal aspects.

Social integration:
- Counselling services can support migrants in social integration by providing information on local communities, cultural adaptation, education systems, health services and other relevant social aspects.

Professional integration:
- Migration counselling can also provide career guidance and job search support. This may include information on local labour markets, recognition of qualifications and continuing vocational training.

Educational guidance:
- Migrants, especially students, can benefit from educational guidance services. This includes information about educational institutions, admission requirements, study opportunities, and funding sources.

Family reunification:
- For migrants who wish to have their families reunited, Migration Counselling can provide assistance with family reunification requirements and procedures.

Crisis intervention:
- In situations where migrants are facing crises or difficult circumstances, migration counselling may also include some form of crisis intervention. This may include psychosocial support and referrals to specialist services.

Healthcare and Social Services:
- Migration counselors can provide information about the health system, access to medical care, social services, and other aspects of health.

Interpreting services:
- As language barriers are a common obstacle for migrants, migration counselling services can also provide interpretation services or refer to relevant resources.

Cultural mediation:

- Cultural mediation is an important part of migration counselling. This includes the mediation of cultural differences, intercultural communication and the understanding of the cultural contexts in the host country.

Residence Permits and Integration:

- Counselling services can help clarify residence status issues and integration steps, including language courses and civil rights.

Migration counselling is crucial to help migrants cope with the multiple challenges of the migration process. Professional counsellors can contribute to a smooth transition and successful integration in the host country.

Needs Assessment Tool

Needs assessment tools in social work are tools and methods used to identify the individual needs, resources, and challenges of clients. These tools help social workers make comprehensive assessments, develop individual plans, and plan appropriate interventions. Examples of needs assessment tools include:

Social history:

- Social history is a standardized method of recording biographical information, social relationships, housing conditions, professional backgrounds, and other relevant aspects of a person's life. It offers a holistic view of the life history and current life circumstances.

Lifeworld-oriented needs analysis:
- This method focuses on understanding the client's living environment and perspective. It takes into account individual experiences, desires, goals and social contexts.

Needs Assessment in Healthcare:
- In health social work, specific needs assessment tools are used to identify the health needs of clients. This can include the recording of physical, mental and social health aspects.

Resource Analysis:
- This approach focuses not only on the client's needs, but also on the client's existing resources and strengths. The analysis includes financial, social, personal and institutional resources.

Assessment tools in child and youth welfare:
- In the work with children and adolescents, special assessment tools are used to assess their development, school situation, family circumstances and emotional well-being.

Disability-related needs assessment:
- When working with people with disabilities, tools are used to identify specific needs in terms of accessibility, assistive technologies, education and employment.

Standardized questionnaires:
- Questionnaires may include standardized questions to assess specific aspects such as mental health, quality of life, or social support. These can provide quantifiable data.

Participatory needs assessment:
- This approach emphasizes the involvement of clients in the needs assessment. It allows clients to identify their own needs, goals and preferences and actively involve them in the planning process.

Crisis Intervention Talks:

- In acute crisis situations, specific conversational techniques are used to identify the immediate needs and security aspects.

Strength- and resource-oriented assessments:

- These assessments focus on identifying a person's strengths and resources in order to drive positive change on that basis.

The choice of the appropriate needs assessment tool depends on the specific requirements of social work practice and the needs of the clients.

Occupational therapy

Occupational therapy is an area of healthcare that aims to help people improve their independence and ability to act in everyday life. Occupational therapists work with people of all ages who have difficulty managing their daily activities due to illness, injury, disability, or other challenges.

Aim of occupational therapy:

- The main goal of occupational therapy is to help people improve their independence and ability to act in everyday activities. This includes areas such as self-sufficiency, work and leisure.

Customization:

- Occupational therapists tailor their interventions individually to the needs of each client. Therapy is designed to take into account the specific challenges and goals of the person.

Assessment and objective:

- Occupational therapists first perform a comprehensive assessment to understand a person's limitations and abilities. Based on this assessment, they work with the client to develop realistic goals for therapy.

Everyday activities:

- A central feature of occupational therapy is the inclusion of everyday activities. These can be basic self-care skills such as eating, dressing and washing, or complex activities such as work or leisure activities.

Motor skills:

- Occupational therapists can work on improving motor skills, including fine and gross motor skills. This may include developing dexterity in handling tools, writing, keying, or other activities.

Sensory Integration:

- In pediatric occupational therapy, work often focuses on sensory integration to help children with sensory processing problems respond better to stimuli from their environment.

Cognitive Abilities:

- Occupational therapists also support the development of cognitive skills such as attention, memory, problem-solving, and organizational skills.

Adaptations to the environment:

- Occupational therapy also includes adapting the environment to promote independence. This may include the modification of living quarters or workplaces.

Psychosocial support:

- Occupational therapists also provide psychosocial support by dealing with the emotional and social aspects of coping with challenges that may accompany health impairments.

Working with different age groups:
- Occupational therapy is used in people of all ages, from children to older adults. The areas of application can be varied, from pediatric developmental disorders to geriatric problems.

Occupational therapy plays a fundamental role in promoting the quality of life of people with health impairments. The interventions aim to support participation in life and the community by strengthening people's skills and resources.

Outpatient Psychiatric Care

Outpatient psychiatric care is a mental health care service. It is aimed at people with mental illness who live at home and need support.

Goals of Outpatient Psychiatric Care:
- Stabilization and improvement of mental health.
- Promotion of self-reliance and self-determination.
- Avoidance or reduction of hospitalizations.
- Support in coping with everyday life and social integration.

Outpatient psychiatric care services:

Psychosocial support: Nurses offer counselling and support to reduce psychosocial stress and improve quality of life.

Medication management: Assistance with medication intake and monitoring of possible side effects.

Help with everyday life: Help with household chores, shopping and other everyday tasks.

Crisis intervention: Rapid help in acute crisis situations to avoid inpatient stays.

Promotion of social contacts: support in participating in social activities and building social networks.

Target groups:

- People with serious mental illnesses such as schizophrenia, mood disorders, anxiety disorders or personality disorders.
- People who return to their home environment after an inpatient stay and need support there.

Team & Collaboration:

- Outpatient psychiatric care is usually performed by qualified nurses such as psychiatric nurses.
- Collaborate with other healthcare stakeholders, such as doctors, therapists, and social workers, to ensure comprehensive care.

Financing:

- The costs for outpatient psychiatric care may be covered by health or long-term care insurance.

Outpatient psychiatric care plays an important role in community-based care for people with mental illnesses. It enables individually tailored support in the familiar environment of those affected.

Paraphrasing

Paraphrasing means reproducing a text or statement in one's own words without altering the meaning. Paraphrasing is an important skill of written communication that is used in various contexts, including academic and professional texts. Paraphrasing can be used to convey complex ideas or information in a clear and understandable way without plagiarism.

Wording:
- When paraphrasing, it is important to change the original choice of words to ensure a clear and original wording. Synonyms can be helpful in maintaining diversity in the language.

Comprehensive Understanding:
- To paraphrase effectively, a deep understanding of the original text is required. This includes understanding the main ideas, key terms, and structure.

Change in sentence structure:
- In addition to changing words, it is often necessary to change the structure of sentences. This includes changing parts of sentences, using different types of sentences, or varying sentence lengths.

Maintaining Relevance:
- The paraphrasing is intended to preserve the original meaning of the text. One should make sure that the reworded passage conveys the same core ideas as the source text.

Summary:
- Paraphrasing can also be a form of summary, where the text is reduced to its most important points without losing the essential meaning.

Adapted wording:
- Paraphrasing requires adapting the wording to one's own writing style. This makes it possible to choose the words and structures so that they fit well into the context of one's own text.

Avoidance of plagiarism:

- Correct paraphrasing prevents plagiarism because it rephrases the text in a way that can be considered work in its own right. However, it is important to cite sources properly when borrowing ideas or information from other texts.

The ability to paraphrase is important in many written contexts, especially academic papers, reports, or other forms of written communication. It helps to demonstrate one's own originality and understanding of the material.

Participation

Participation refers to the active and equal participation of people in social, political, economic or cultural processes and decisions. It is about individuals and groups having the opportunity to express their opinions, participate in decision-making processes and participate in social life.

Political participation:

- This refers to the participation of citizens in political processes and decisions. These include the right to vote, participation in political assemblies, participation in citizens' initiatives and active participation in political organisations.

Social Participation:

- Social participation includes the participation of people in social activities and community life. This may include volunteering, membership in social groups, participation in events, and promoting solidarity and social inclusion.

Economic Participation:

- This refers to people's participation in economic life. This includes the opportunity to participate in the labour market, make economic decisions, be an entrepreneur or participate in cooperatives.

Education and participation:

- Education plays an important role in fostering participation by providing people with the necessary skills and knowledge to actively participate in various aspects of life.

Cultural Participation:

- Cultural participation refers to active participation in cultural activities. This can include participating in artistic events, promoting cultural exchange, and co-creating cultural content.

Participation of minorities:

- An inclusive society promotes the participation of minorities to ensure that all members of the community have equal rights and opportunities to express themselves and participate in decision-making.

Participation in the digital world:

- Digitalisation has enabled new forms of participation, such as participation in online discussions, sharing information on social media or using digital platforms to participate in decision-making processes.

Participatory Research:

- In academia, participatory research (also known as participatory research methods) can mean the active involvement of people in the research process to ensure that their perspectives and experiences are adequately taken into account.

Participation of young people:

- The participation of young people in decision-making processes, whether in schools, communities or at national level, is an important aspect of youth development and democratic development.

Participatory urban development:
- In urban planning processes, citizens are increasingly actively involved in shaping their urban environment by contributing ideas, participating in workshops and participating in decisions on urban development projects.

Participation is a prerequisite for a functioning democracy and an inclusive society. It promotes self-determination, empowerment and shared responsibility for the common good. Effective participation requires open communication, access to information, society's willingness to accept diversity of opinion, and the creation of structures that facilitate participation.

Participation in cultural life

Participation in cultural life refers to the right and opportunity of every individual to actively participate in cultural activities and to use cultural resources. Cultural participation is a central aspect of social inclusion and promotes the integration of people into the cultural diversity of a society.

Access to culture:
- Cultural participation presupposes that people have access to various cultural offerings, be it in the fields of art, music, theatre, literature, film or other forms of expression.

Cultural Education:
- The opportunity to participate in cultural life also includes cultural education. This includes access to educational

institutions that teach cultural skills and the promotion of lifelong learning.

Valuing diversity:

- Cultural participation recognizes and values the diversity of cultural expressions. This includes an appreciation of different cultural backgrounds, traditions, and creative expressions.

Cultural Integration:

- Participation in cultural life promotes the cultural integration of people into a society. It enables individuals to engage with and participate in the cultural identity of their environment.

Accessibility in culture:

- Cultural participation requires accessibility, not only physically, but also in terms of language, information and technology. All people should have equal access to cultural events and information.

Cultural identity:

- Participation in cultural life enables people to cultivate and express their own cultural identity. This can be done by participating in cultural events, traditions and rituals.

Free speech:

- Cultural participation is linked to the right to freedom of expression. Cultural expressions, whether through art, music, or literature, offer people the opportunity to share their ideas and perspectives.

Cultural Communities:

- Participation in cultural life includes participation in cultural communities. This may mean being active in local arts or cultural organizations, or participating in cultural events.

Cultural Justice:

- Cultural participation is also linked to cultural justice. This means ensuring that all people, regardless of their background, have equal opportunities to participate in cultural activities.

Promoting cultural diversity:

- Cultural participation promotes the recognition and appreciation of cultural diversity. This helps to break down prejudices and promote understanding between different cultural groups.

Cultural heritage:

- Participation in cultural life enables people to preserve and pass on their cultural heritage. This can be done by participating in cultural festivals, events, and traditions.

Cultural participation for all age groups:

- Cultural participation should be accessible to people of all ages, including children, young people, adults and the elderly. Cultural activities should be intergenerational.

Cultural participation is not only an individual right, but also an essential element of an inclusive and diverse society. It promotes creative exchange, strengthens social cohesion and contributes to the development of a vibrant and dynamic cultural landscape.

Participation planning

Participation planning is a strategic process that aims to ensure the full inclusion and active participation of people in different areas of life. Participation planning often takes place in the context of social work and social support for people with special needs, such as people with disabilities or people at risk of social exclusion.

Market analysis:

- Participation planning often begins with a thorough needs analysis. It identifies what support and resources a person needs to actively participate in social life.

Individual objectives:

- Planning focuses on individual goals and needs. These can be educational goals, career goals, social goals, or other aspects of life that encourage participation and involvement.

Person-centered approach:

- Participation planning takes a person-centred approach that focuses on the wishes, preferences and strengths of the person concerned. The individual contribution to planning is important.

Interdisciplinary cooperation:

- Often, participation planning requires the collaboration of various professionals, including social workers, health care providers, education experts, and others, to get a comprehensive picture of a person's needs.

Resource Mobilization:

- Participation planning involves identifying and mobilizing resources that can support individual goals. These can include financial resources, social support, educational resources, and more.

Participation of the data subject:

- The person concerned or the group of persons for whom the participation planning is carried out should be actively involved in the planning process. This includes the type of support, preferences and setting goals.

Implementation strategies:

- Participation planning develops concrete implementation strategies to achieve the identified goals. This may include the provision of specific services, training, or other supportive measures.

Monitoring and evaluation:
- Progress is regularly monitored and evaluated to ensure that planned actions are effective and meet individual needs. Adjustments will be made as needed.

Long-term perspective:
- Participation planning often has a long-term perspective. It is about not only meeting short-term needs, but also defining long-term goals to ensure long-term participation.

Rights and self-determination:
- The planning takes into account the rights of the data subject and strives for self-determination. This means that the person has as much control as possible over their own life choices.

Cooperation with community and institutions:
- Participation planning often requires collaboration with communities and institutions to create an inclusive environment and remove barriers to participation.

Crisis management and contingency planning:
- Participation planning can also include aspects of crisis management and contingency planning to ensure that participation in social life is supported even in difficult situations.

Participation planning is a dynamic and flexible process that aims to meet individual needs and goals and ensure that all people can participate equally in social life.

Participatory orientation

Participatory orientation refers to an orientation of processes, institutions or projects that aims to promote the active participation and co-determination of the persons or groups concerned. This approach seeks to democratize decision-making processes and actions by ensuring that those affected by certain decisions or actions have the opportunity to contribute their perspectives and exert influence.

Inclusive decision-making processes:
- Participatory orientation means keeping decision-making processes open and ensuring that different stakeholders and stakeholders are invited to contribute their opinions, concerns and suggestions.

Empowerment:
- The participatory approach aims to promote the self-determination and empowerment of the individuals concerned by giving them the opportunity to actively participate in decisions that affect their living conditions.

Transparency and information:
- An important prerequisite for participatory orientation is the provision of clear information about processes, decisions and their effects. Transparency creates the basis for informed participation.

Dialogue and communication:
- The exchange of information and dialogue between the participants are central to the participation orientation. This can take the form of public discussions, workshops, citizens' panels or other participatory formats.

Diversity of perspectives:
- Participatory orientation strives to include a diversity of perspectives and experiences. This includes taking into

account different social, cultural, ethnic and gender backgrounds.

Partnership-based cooperation:

- Instead of top-down decision-making structures, the participatory orientation promotes partnership-based cooperation between the decision-makers and the individuals or groups concerned.

Orientation towards the common good:

- Participatory orientation is geared towards shaping decisions and measures in the interests of the common good. This means that stakeholders work together to develop solutions that are beneficial to society as a whole.

Participatory Evaluation:

- After the implementation of measures or projects, a participatory evaluation is carried out, in which the affected individuals or groups are actively involved in order to assess the impact and make possible adjustments.

Consideration of vulnerability:

- Participatory orientation takes into account the different positions of power and vulnerabilities of those involved. It aims to ensure that disadvantaged groups also have a voice.

Legitimacy and Acceptance:

- The legitimacy of decisions is strengthened by a participatory orientation, as they are more accepted in society through the broad involvement of stakeholders.

Participation is of great importance in various fields such as politics, administration, education, social work and corporate management. It promotes democratic values, strengthens the trust of stakeholders and leads to more sustainable and effective solutions.

Participatory research

Participatory research, also called participatory research methods or participatory research approaches, is a research approach in which those who are affected by the research are actively involved in the research process. This approach aims to take into account the perspectives and experiences of stakeholders and ensure that research produces relevant, practical and socially equitable outcomes.

Stakeholder involvement:
- Participatory research aims to actively involve stakeholders in the research process. These can be community members, patients, students, staff, or other groups that have a direct connection to the research topic.

Common definition of the research objective:
- The research question and objectives are defined jointly by the researchers and the participants. This ensures that the research is relevant to everyone and addresses the needs of those affected.

Participatory data collection:
- Data collection is carried out in a participatory manner. This may mean that participants collect data themselves, participate in interviews, discuss in focus groups, or are otherwise actively involved in the research process.

Dialogue and communication:
- The exchange of information and dialogue between researchers and stakeholders are at the heart of participatory research. This fosters open communication and builds trust.

Importance of experiential knowledge:
- Participatory research recognises the importance of the experiential knowledge of those involved. This knowledge is

considered equivalent to scientific knowledge and helps to gain a broader perspective on the research topic.

Empowerment of those involved:

- Through active participation in the research process, the participants are to be empowered. This means that they can influence research and use the results to bring about positive changes in their lives.

Cooperation on an equal footing:

- Participatory research promotes equal cooperation between researchers and stakeholders. It avoids that researchers take a higher position, and instead emphasizes partnership and joint decision-making.

Adaptability of the research process:

- Participatory research is characterized by a high degree of adaptability. The research process can be adapted according to needs and developments to meet the changing needs of stakeholders.

Ethics and Responsibility:

- Participatory research emphasizes ethical principles and responsibility towards those involved. This includes the protection of their privacy, the disclosure of research objectives and transparent communication.

Application-oriented results:

- The goal of participatory research is often to develop application-oriented results that can be directly translated into practice. This helps to increase the relevance and practicability of the research results.

Participatory research is applied in a wide range of disciplines, including social sciences, health sciences, education, environmental research, and many others. It provides an opportunity to expand the reach and influence of research and ensure that the voices of those who are often marginalized are heard.

Partnership

Partnership in a social or professional context refers to cooperation in which all parties involved are seen as equal partners. It's about building an equal relationship where the needs, perspectives, and contributions of all parties are respected and taken into account.

Mutual Respect:
- Partnership is based on mutual respect for the skills, experiences and opinions of all parties involved. Each party is seen as an important contributor to cooperation.

Equality:
- Equality is a central principle of partnership. All partners have the right to participate in decisions on an equal footing and to influence the course of cooperation.

Shared decision-making:
- In partnership-based relationships, the decision-making process is shaped jointly. This includes involving all relevant stakeholders in the process to ensure that different perspectives are taken into account.

Transparent communication:
- Clear and open communication is crucial for partnership. All stakeholders share information and communicate their needs and expectations to build understanding.

Sharing of responsibility:
- Partnership entails shared responsibility for the goals and tasks of cooperation. Tasks are divided based on each partner's skills and resources.

Flexibility and adaptability:
- Partnership relationships are flexible and adapt to changing conditions. This allows partners to respond to challenges and find solutions together.

Recognizing Diversity:
- Partnership respects the diversity of the actors involved. This includes cultural, social and individual differences and promotes inclusive cooperation.

Long-term perspective:
- Partnership is often geared towards long-term cooperation. It's about building relationships that go beyond individual projects and are based on trust and continuity.

Goal orientation:
- Partnership relationships are designed to achieve common goals. All stakeholders work together to achieve outcomes that benefit the entire partnership.

Partnership in different contexts:
- Partnership is applied in various contexts, be it in social services, educational institutions, businesses, between government and civil society, or in international cooperation.

Partnership fosters positive and sustainable cooperation based on respect, equality and shared responsibility. In the field of social services and social work, partnership is often a key principle to ensure effective support and interventions.

Peers

The term "peers" refers to people who are on a similar level, often in terms of experiences, affiliations, or life situations. The term is used in different contexts and can have different meanings. The following are some of the most common uses of the term "peers":

Peer Group:
- In youth and social research, "peers" often refers to peers or members of the same age group. The peer group plays an important role in adolescent development, as peers have an influence on behavior, attitudes, and social identity.

Peer Support:
- In the field of mental health and rehabilitation, "peer support" refers to the sharing of experiences and resources between individuals who have experienced similar challenges, illnesses, or life situations. Peer supporters can offer a unique perspective and understanding.

Peer Education:
- The term is also used in education, especially peer education. Here, students take on the role of teachers or advisors for their peers. This can help information be better understood and accepted when conveyed by peers.

Peer review:
- In scientific research, "peer review" refers to the process by which scientific papers are reviewed by experts in the same field before being published in scientific journals. These experts are considered peers.

Peer Coaching:
- In the coaching environment, "peer coaching" can mean that colleagues or peers coach each other to improve professional skills or overcome professional challenges.

Peer-to-Peer Networks:
- In technology, peer-to-peer (P2P) refers to a decentralized form of data transmission in which computers communicate directly with each other, without a central server. This concept is also used in other areas to mean on an equal level or directly between people.

Peer pressure:
- This term describes the influence that peers can exert on a person's behavior, decisions, or attitudes. Peer pressure can be positive or negative.

Peer Recognition:
- In organizations, "peer recognition" refers to the recognition and appreciation of achievements by colleagues at the same hierarchical level.

The use of the term "peers" depends heavily on the context. In many cases, it stands for equality, shared experiences, and a shared perspective.

Pension Office

The Pension Office is an institution responsible for providing services and assistance to people with disabilities. They can have different names, such as "pension office", "pension authority" or similar names.

Determination of disability:
- The pension office is often responsible for determining the degree of disability (GdB). The GdB provides information about the severity of the impairment and can form the basis for various benefits.

Severely disabled person's pass:
- On the basis of the determination of the disability, the pension office usually issues the severely disabled person's

pass. This card grants certain rights and benefits, such as tax breaks, parking permits or priority employment services.

Identification of markers:

- In addition to the GdB, the pension office can also identify marks that are entered in the severely disabled person's pass. These can mean additional entitlements and benefits, such as the right to take an accompanying person with you.

Integration assistance:

- In some countries and regions, the pension office is also responsible for granting integration assistance. This can be, for example, financial support for disability-friendly conversions or assistance services.

Advice and information:

- The pension office often offers advice and information on various services and assistance for people with disabilities. This may also include clarifying questions about legal claims.

Determination of reduced earning capacity:

- In some countries, the pension office may also be responsible for determining a reduction in earning capacity. This has an impact on pension insurance benefits.

Participation benefits:

- The pension office may grant benefits for participation in working life or for participation in community life. This may include rehabilitation, assistive technology or other measures.

Levels of care:

- In some countries, the pension office also has a role to play in determining care levels and related support, especially in the area of long-term care insurance.

The exact structure and responsibilities of the pension offices may vary. People with disabilities and their relatives can contact the local pension office for information about

the services and assistance available to meet their
individual needs.

Physiotherapy

Physiotherapy, also known as physiotherapy, is a form of
medical therapy that aims to improve or restore people's
physical functioning, mobility and quality of life.
Physiotherapy is carried out by trained professionals, the
physiotherapists.

Evaluation and diagnosis:
- Physical therapists perform a comprehensive assessment to
  identify the causes of physical discomfort or dysfunction.
  This includes assessing movement, muscle strength, joint
  function, and other relevant aspects.

Creation of an individual treatment plan:
- Based on the assessment, physical therapists develop an
  individualized treatment plan for each patient. This plan
  may include exercises, manual therapy, electrotherapy, heat
  or cold therapy, and other techniques.

Movement exercises and rehabilitation:
- The core aspect of physiotherapy is movement exercises
  that aim to strengthen muscles, improve joint function and
  increase flexibility. Rehabilitation after injuries or surgery is
  also an important area.

Manual therapy:
- Physical therapists often use manual techniques such as
  massage, mobilization, and manipulation to relieve muscle
  tension, mobilize joints, and promote blood circulation.

Pain management:

- Physical therapists often work to improve pain symptoms, whether by using specific techniques, improving posture, or teaching self-management strategies.

Respiratory therapy:

- In certain cases, such as breathing difficulties or lung disease, physical therapists may use breathing techniques and breathing exercises to improve respiratory function.

Gait analysis:

- Gait analysis is an important part of physiotherapy to identify gait disorders and make appropriate interventions.

Instructions for self-help:

- A central aspect of physiotherapy is the training of patients in self-help techniques. This may include performing specific exercises at home, adjusting lifestyle habits, or avoiding improper strain.

Prevention and health promotion:

- Physical therapists work not only to treat existing problems, but also to prevent injuries and promote overall health and well-being.

Collaboration in an interdisciplinary team:

- Physiotherapists often work as part of an interdisciplinary team, especially when it comes to the rehabilitation of patients with complex medical conditions. Collaborating with doctors, nurses, and other professionals is crucial.

Physical therapy is used in a variety of contexts, including hospitals, rehabilitation centers, outpatient practices, care facilities, sports teams, and many others. It plays an important role in restoring and improving the quality of life of people with various health problems.

Polity

The community refers to a group of people who live in a geographical area and share common interests, values, and resources. It goes beyond individual households and encompasses the social, cultural, economic and political life of a community.

Shared Identity and Values:
- Communities develop a common identity through shared values, traditions, norms and customs. These common elements foster a sense of belonging and togetherness.

Social Capital:
- Social capital refers to the social relationships, networks, and cooperation within a community. Strong social capital fosters trust, collaboration, and mutual exchange of resources.

Participation and commitment:
- The active participation and engagement of members in various social, cultural and political activities are crucial for the strengthening of the community. This may include participation in events, initiatives, or community projects.

Local resources and services:
- Communities have local resources, whether in the form of educational institutions, health services, shops, or cultural institutions. The provision and access to these resources affects the quality of life in a community.

Community Organizations:
- Community organisations, such as citizens' initiatives, sports clubs, religious groups or neighbourhood associations, play a role in organising activities, promoting cohesion and representing interests.

Cultural diversity:
- Cultural diversity in a community can be enriching. The respectful treatment of different cultural backgrounds and traditions promotes understanding and harmony.

Neighbourhood relations:
- The quality of relations between neighbours contributes significantly to the quality of life. A strong sense of neighborliness can foster safety, social support, and a sense of security.

Citizen Participation and Local Politics:
- The participation of citizens in local political processes and decisions is an important aspect of the community. Citizens can exert influence by participating in municipal council meetings, citizens' initiatives or other forms of co-determination.

Crisis management:
- In times of crisis, whether due to natural disasters, economic challenges or other stresses, communities play a crucial role in solidarity, support and recovery.

Community Development and Planning:
- Community development and planning refers to processes in which the members of a community collectively decide on the future of their environment and plan actions.

Digitalization and community:
- In modern times, digitalization also plays a role in the community, whether through online platforms, social media, or digital resources that promote exchange and communication in the community.

Community empowerment helps to create a vibrant, supportive and sustainable environment for people. A well-functioning community promotes social justice, inclusion, and the well-being of its members.

Poverty and social work

Poverty and social work are closely related subject areas, as social work often aims to support people in precarious life situations, including poverty, and improve their quality of life.

Poverty:
- Poverty is a complex social phenomenon that encompasses not only the lack of financial resources, but also the lack of access to education, health care, adequate housing and social participation. Poverty can have individual, family and societal dimensions.

Causes of poverty:
- Poverty can be caused by various factors, including unemployment, inadequate education, health problems, discrimination, social injustice, and structural problems in society.

Social Work Against Poverty:
- Social work plays a crucial role in supporting people affected by poverty. It aims to address individual and structural causes of poverty and promote social justice.

Social Work in the Field of Poverty Prevention:
- Preventive social work measures can aim to minimise the causes of poverty by, for example, providing educational support, professional qualifications and job-search support.

Social Work in Poverty Reduction:
- In cases where people are already affected by poverty, social work offers support in coping with acute problems. This includes the provision of financial assistance, shelter, food assistance, and counseling services.

Empowerment and participation:

- Social work also strives to strengthen the self-determination and participation of people in precarious life situations. This means giving them the tools and resources to actively improve their living conditions.

Social Change and Advocacy:

- Social work often engages in societal change and advocacy to identify and influence structural issues that contribute to the emergence and perpetuation of poverty.

Networking:

- Social work often works with other organisations, government agencies and communities to jointly ensure comprehensive and sustainable support for people in vulnerable situations.

The link between poverty and social work highlights the importance of a holistic approach to tackling social challenges. Social work seeks not only to alleviate the symptoms of poverty, but also to address the root causes in order to promote long-term change.

Prevention

Prevention refers to measures taken to prevent or minimize the occurrence of disease, injury, or other undesirable conditions. The focus is on identifying potential risk factors, early intervention, and preventing the onset of health problems.

Primary prevention:

- Primary prevention aims to prevent illness or injury before it even occurs. This can be done through education, vaccinations, behavioral changes, and other measures that reduce the risk.

Secondary:

- Secondary prevention focuses on stopping or slowing the progression of disease at an early stage. This includes screening and early detection programs to identify diseases at an early, treatable stage.

Tertiary prevention:

- Tertiary prevention refers to measures taken to minimize the impact of an existing illness or injury and prevent relapses. Rehabilitation programs are an example of tertiary prevention.

Health promotion:

- Health promotion is a broader approach that aims to promote overall health and well-being. This can be achieved through education, lifestyle interventions, access to healthy foods, promotion of physical activity, and other interventions.

Education and awareness-raising:

- An important component of prevention is educating the public about health risks, protective measures and healthy lifestyle habits. Raising awareness helps people make informed decisions about their health.

Vaccinations:

- Vaccinations are an effective means of primary prevention and help prevent infectious diseases. They help to stop or minimize the spread of pathogens.

Preventive health check-ups:

- Regular health check-ups and screenings allow for early detection of diseases before they cause symptoms. This facilitates timely intervention.

Lifestyle Changes:

- Promoting healthy lifestyle habits, such as a balanced diet, regular physical activity, adequate sleep, and stress management, goes a long way in preventing it.

Occupational health and safety measures:

- In work environments, preventive measures are important to prevent injuries and work-related illnesses. This may include the provision of protective equipment, training, and safe working practices.

Health policy:

- Government and community policies can have a significant impact on prevention. This includes laws that promote access to health-promoting resources, as well as measures to reduce environmental triggers of disease.

Prevention is an integral part of the healthcare system and helps reduce the burden of illness and injury. A holistic approach, encompassing both individual responsibility and societal action, is crucial to promoting the health of the population.

Pre-vocational training measure

The pre-vocational training measure is a measure that supports young people in preparing for vocational training. It is aimed at young people who need special support and encouragement to develop the knowledge, skills and personal competences necessary to enter the world of work. The following are some of the key elements

179

associated with pre-vocational training:

Target group:
- The target group of the pre-vocational training are young people who have difficulties in making the transition from school to vocational training. These include, for example, school leavers without a school leaving certificate, young people with learning difficulties or social problems.

Individual support:
- It is characterized by individual support for the participants. The measures are adapted to the specific needs, abilities and development potential of the young people.

Career Orientation:
- An important part is vocational orientation. Young people gain insights into various professional fields in order to better understand their interests and inclinations.

Teaching key qualifications:
- In addition to technical content, the pre-vocational attaches great importance to teaching key qualifications, such as teamwork, communication skills, self-organisation and conflict management.

Practical experience:
- It enables the young people to gain practical experience through internships in companies. This gives them the opportunity to test and deepen their skills in real work environments.

Continuing education in schools:
- Depending on needs, school-based continuing education measures can be part of it. This can include both improving basic skills and preparing for a specific education.

Socio-pedagogical support:
- The pre-vocational training often includes socio-pedagogical support to support young people with personal and social challenges. This can also include fostering self-confidence and personal responsibility.

180

Consulting and Coaching:
- Young people receive counselling and coaching to clarify their professional goals, develop individual perspectives and develop their potential.

Preparation for applications and interviews:
- Another important aspect of pre-vocational training is the preparation for the application process. This includes writing job applications, training for job interviews and generally teaching job application skills.

Integration into the labour market:
- The main objective of the pre-vocational training is the integration of young people into the labour market or the transition to qualified vocational training.

The exact structure of the pre-vocational training can vary depending on regional conditions, the institutions responsible for the measures and individual needs. However, it plays an important role in enabling young people with special needs to make a successful entry into the world of work.

Psychotherapy

Psychotherapy is a form of treatment for mental disorders, emotional problems, and interpersonal difficulties with the help of conversational methods. A specially trained psychotherapist conducts the therapy to help patients better understand their thoughts, feelings, behavioral patterns, and interpersonal relationships and bring about positive changes.

Targeted Process:

- Psychotherapy is a goal-oriented process that aims to identify, understand, and manage specific problems. Goals can range from reducing symptoms to improving quality of life.

Confidentiality:

- A central principle of psychotherapy is confidentiality. Therapeutic sessions are confidential, and information about the patient is not shared without consent.

Therapeutic Relationship:

- The relationship between the therapist and the patient plays a crucial role. A supportive and understanding therapeutic relationship creates a safe environment for the exploration of thoughts and feelings.

Different therapeutic approaches:

- There are several therapeutic approaches used in psychotherapy, including cognitive-behavioral therapy, psychoanalytic therapy, humanistic therapy, systemic therapy, and others. The choice depends on the individual needs of the patient and the orientation of the therapist.

Conversation-based:

- Psychotherapy is based on conversations between therapist and patient. Through conversation, thoughts, emotions, and behavioral patterns are explored to bring about change.

Self-reflection:

- Psychotherapy promotes self-reflection by encouraging people to reflect on their own thought patterns, beliefs, and behaviors.

Problem solving:

- An important aspect of psychotherapy is to help the patient identify problems and develop positive solutions. This may include developing new coping strategies and fostering self-management skills.

Duration and frequency:

- The duration and frequency of psychotherapy may vary depending on the patient's needs. Sometimes short-term therapy is sufficient for acute problems, while other patients may benefit from long-term support.

Intercultural Competence:

- Psychotherapists strive to develop intercultural competence in order to better understand the diversity of patients and respond appropriately to their needs.

Evaluation and Feedback:

- The progress of therapy is regularly evaluated and patients have the opportunity to provide feedback. This makes it possible to check the effectiveness of the therapy and make adjustments if necessary.

It should be noted that psychotherapy can be supportive not only for mental disorders, but also for various life challenges and personal growth. The success of a therapy often depends on the cooperation between therapist and patient.

Public relief

Social support refers to various forms of help, support and care that people in difficult life situations receive in order to promote their social participation and improve their living conditions. This support can be individual, family or community and is often an integral part of social services and social policy.

Demand orientation:

- Social support is needs-based and based on individual or family needs. This may include material, financial, health, or emotional support.

Livelihood:

- A fundamental function of social assistance is to ensure the minimum subsistence level. This may include financial assistance in the form of social benefits, food assistance, or assistance with rent and energy costs.

Labour market integration:

- For people who have difficulties in accessing the labour market, social support can include measures for professional integration and qualification. This may include training programs, job placement, and vocational rehabilitation.

Health care:

- Social assistance also includes access to health care. This may include providing health insurance, medical care, and assistance in addressing health challenges.

Education and training:

- The promotion of education and training is an important part of social support. This may include financial support for education expenses, tutoring, or access to continuing education.

Family support:

- Families, especially single parents and large families, often receive special support. These include, for example, child benefit, family-related benefits and support in reconciling family and career.

Disability support:

- People with disabilities receive social support to promote their participation in social life. This includes financial benefits, barrier-free access and special support services.

Senior support:

- Older people receive support to lead a self-determined life in old age. These include long-term care services, old-age pensions, barrier-free housing and social activities.

Social Counselling:

- Social counselling is often an integral part of social support. Counselling centres offer support for personal, family or professional challenges.

Crisis intervention:

- Social support also includes crisis intervention measures. This may include emergency assistance in emergency situations, such as natural disasters or personal crises.

Social integration:

- The promotion of social inclusion is an overarching objective of social support. This includes measures for participation in social, cultural and community life.

Social support is diverse and is provided by state institutions, non-profit organizations, charities and other actors. It plays a crucial role in reducing social inequalities and enabling equal opportunities for people in different life situations.

Quality

Quality management (QM) is a systematic approach to planning, directing, and improving processes, products, and services in organizations to ensure customer satisfaction and efficiency.

Quality standards:

- Quality management involves setting clear quality standards that define the expectations of products or services. These standards can be industry-specific or set by international standards such as ISO 9001.

Quality:

- Organizations set quality goals to ensure that quality standards are met or exceeded. These goals should be measurable, realistic, and aligned with customer needs.

Process:

- QM involves identifying, documenting, and monitoring business processes. By optimising processes, efficiency gains and quality improvements can be achieved.

Customer orientation:

- An essential principle of quality management is customer orientation. Organizations should understand the needs and expectations of their customers and ensure that their products or services meet those requirements.

Risk management:

- QM involves identifying and assessing risks that could affect quality. Measures to avoid or mitigate risks are implemented.

Documentation and Reporting:

- All relevant processes and procedures should be documented. This enables transparent communication within the organization and provides a basis for audits and reviews.

Quality Inspection & Measurement:

- Regular monitoring and measurement of quality performance is critical. This can be done through audits, inspections, interviews, and other methods.

Continuous Improvement:

- A central principle of quality management is continuous improvement. Organizations should systematically look for ways to improve their processes, products, and services.

Training & Development:

- Employees should be trained in the principles of quality management. This includes both technical training and training to foster a culture of quality and develop skills for continuous improvement.

Certification and Accreditation:

- Some organizations seek certification to international standards such as ISO 9001 to validate their quality practices. This can build trust with customers and stakeholders.

Use customer feedback:

- Customer feedback is valuable for quality management. Organizations should respond to customer complaints, leverage positive feedback, and continuously evaluate customer satisfaction.

Quality management is critical in many industries to ensure competitiveness, meet customer demands, and ensure long-term success. It is a dynamic process based on continuous monitoring, evaluation and adaptation.

Rehabilitation

Rehabilitation is a central term in social work and refers to the process of restoring or improving skills, functions and quality of life of people who are impaired by illness, injury, addiction or other life circumstances. The main goal of rehabilitation in social work is to support people in leading as independent and self-determined a life as possible. Examples of rehabilitation in social work can be varied and depend on the individual needs of the clients:

Physical rehabilitation:
- An accident victim who has suffered a serious injury could receive physiotherapy rehabilitation to restore mobility and strength.

Addiction Treatment:
- A person who is addicted to alcohol or drugs could participate in a rehabilitation program that provides medical, psychological, and social support to overcome addiction.

Vocational rehabilitation:
- Persons with disabilities could receive support for vocational rehabilitation in order to develop or retrain their professional skills in order to promote their integration into the labour market.

Psychosocial rehabilitation:
- Individuals with mental illness could participate in programs aimed at strengthening their social skills, self-confidence, and ability to socialize.

Rehabilitation in the penitentiary system:
- Prisoners serving a prison sentence could go through social rehabilitation programs to support their reintegration into society and reduce the likelihood of recidivism.

Rehabilitation of children and adolescents:
- Children and adolescents who have had traumatic experiences due to neglect or abuse could participate in

therapy programs to strengthen their emotional and social skills.

These examples show how diverse rehabilitation in social work can be and how it can be adapted to different needs and life situations. The approach should always be holistic, taking into account physical, psychological, social and professional aspects equally.

Rehabilitation Management

Rehabilitation management refers to the coordinated and systematic planning, organization and monitoring of rehabilitation activities. In social work, rehabilitation management plays a crucial role in ensuring that clients' needs are effectively met and that they receive the best possible support in restoring their quality of life.

Market analysis:
- A thorough assessment of the client's individual needs is the starting point for rehabilitation management. This may include medical, psychosocial, occupational, and other aspects.

Goal Setting and Goal Planning:
- Together with the client, realistic and achievable goals for rehabilitation are determined. These goals can relate to different areas of life, such as health, social integration or professional reintegration.

Resource coordination:

- Rehabilitation management involves the coordination of various resources, including medical services, therapists, social workers, professional trainers, and other professionals. The cooperation of these resources ensures comprehensive support.

Monitoring and evaluation:

- The client's progress is continuously monitored and evaluated. This allows rehabilitation plans to be adapted according to the client's changing needs and progress.

Interdisciplinary cooperation:

- Rehabilitation management often requires the collaboration of different professionals from different disciplines. This could include doctors, psychologists, social workers, physical therapists, and others working together to implement the rehabilitation plan.

Family & Network Integration:

- Involving family and social networking is often crucial. Rehabilitation management should ensure that supportive caregivers are actively involved in the process to promote the sustainability of rehabilitation.

Continuity and aftercare:

- Rehabilitation management does not end with the achievement of the set goals. Long-term follow-up is crucial to ensure that the progress made is maintained and the client is supported in their quality of life in the long term.

Rehabilitation management requires careful planning, flexibility, and a resource-oriented approach to ensure the best possible support for people in rehabilitation processes.

Resocialization

Resocialization refers to the process of reintegrating people who have committed crimes into society. The aim of rehabilitation is to enable those affected to lead a life free of punishment and independent responsibility. This process plays an important role in the penitentiary system and in social work.

Individual needs analysis:
- Every offender has individual needs, challenges, and strengths. A comprehensive analysis of these aspects is crucial in order to create a tailor-made rehabilitation plan.

Education and vocational rehabilitation:
- Education and vocational qualifications play a central role in rehabilitation. Education and training programmes help people to acquire or improve their professional skills, which increases their chances in the labour market.

Therapeutic interventions:
- Psychological and social support is often necessary to address the underlying causes of criminal behavior. Therapeutic interventions, such as cognitive behavioral therapy or addiction treatment, can be part of the rehabilitation process.

Social integration:
- Resocialization aims at full integration into the community. This includes fostering social skills, participating in social activities, and creating support networks.

Restorative Justice:
- One approach used in rehabilitation is restorative justice. This approach emphasizes reparation for the damage done and accountability to victims as key components of criminal justice.

Aftercare and support:

- After release from prison, continuous follow-up and support is crucial to ensure successful reintegration. This may include mentoring programs, housing assistance, and job search assistance.

Social acceptance and reduction of stigmatization:

- Rehabilitation requires not only the efforts of the individual, but also the acceptance and support of society. Stigma and prejudice against former offenders can make it difficult to reintegrate, so education and awareness-raising are important.

  Rehabilitation is a complex process that requires close cooperation between prisons, social workers, psychosocial services, educational institutions and society. A holistic approach that takes into account individual needs and context is crucial to fostering sustainable positive change.

Resilience

Resilience refers to a person's ability to adapt to stresses, crises or difficult life situations, to recover from them and to emerge stronger from them. In social work, fostering resilience is an important approach to helping people build their psychological resilience and better cope with life's challenges.

Resilience factors:

- Resilience is based on various factors that affect a person's ability to cope with stress. These include social support, emotional intelligence, self-efficacy (belief in one's own ability to act), a positive attitude and the ability to solve problems.

Stress management:

- Resilience includes the ability to manage stressors and deal with them constructively. This may include developing effective coping strategies, such as seeking social support, setting realistic goals, and embracing change.

Homeostasis:

- Resilient people are good at regulating their emotions and have the ability to calm themselves down and focus on positive aspects, even in difficult situations.

Flexibility:

- Resilient individuals show a high degree of adaptability and flexibility. They can adapt to new circumstances, find alternative solutions and learn from experience.

Social support:

- A strong social network and supportive relationships are critical to resilience. The ability to receive support from others and to be supportive yourself helps reduce stress.

Acceptance of change:

- Resilient people are able to accept change and adapt to new circumstances. This includes the ability to learn from failures and see them as opportunities for personal growth.

Self-reflection:

- The capacity for self-reflection allows resilient people to understand their own reactions and thought patterns. This supports them in making positive changes in their thinking and behavior.

In social work, fostering resilience is an important part of interventions, especially when it comes to supporting people in stressful life situations. By strengthening resilience, people can better cope with life's challenges and increase their ability to cope independently.

Resource orientation

Resource orientation is a central approach in social work that aims to identify, promote and use the existing strengths and potentials of individuals and communities. Instead of focusing exclusively on deficits and problems, the focus is on the positive resources available to people.

Strengths-based perspective:
- Resource orientation is based on a strengths-based perspective, which assumes that each person has individual strengths, skills, and resources. These positive elements are identified, acknowledged and included in the aid and development process.

Empowerment:
- The resource-oriented approach aims to empower people by strengthening their skills and competencies. By promoting self-efficacy and self-determination, individuals should be able to shape their lives positively.

Collaborative work:
- Resource orientation fosters collaboration between social workers, clients and other relevant actors. Together, goals are identified, and strategies are developed to make the best use of existing resources.

Networking and community work:
- The view of resources refers not only to individual strengths, but also to the resources within families, communities and networks. Strengthening social bonds and community resources is an important aspect.

Solution orientation:
- The resource orientation emphasizes solution-oriented approaches. Instead of focusing on problems, concrete steps are taken together with the clients to bring about positive change.

Appreciation of diversity:

- Resource orientation takes into account the diversity of resources that are available in different cultures, life contexts and individual life stories. Appreciating this diversity is crucial.

Preventive approach:

- A resource-oriented approach can also be used preventively to strengthen existing resources and prevent potential problems before they worsen.

Resource orientation in social work helps to ensure that support and interventions can be better tailored to the individual needs of the clients. By focusing on strengths and resources, a positive basis for change and development is created.

Salutogenesis

Salutogenesis is a concept developed by Aaron Antonovsky that focuses on the emergence of health rather than the causes of disease. The term "salutogenesis" is derived from the Latin words "salus" (health) and "genesis" (origination). In contrast to pathogenesis, which deals with the causes of disease, salutogenesis studies the factors that contribute to the emergence and maintenance of health.

Sense of Coherence:

- A central concept in salutogenesis is the sense of coherence, which Antonovsky defined as a person's fundamental orientation towards their environment. The sense of coherence is made up of three components: comprehensibility (the ability to understand and explain life events), manageability (the belief that one is capable of dealing with challenges), and significance (the belief that challenges are worth dealing with).

Health Promoting Resources:

- Salutogenesis emphasizes the importance of health-promoting resources that include individual, social, and community factors. These include personal skills, social support, education, economic resources, and cultural influences.

Resistance Resources:

- Another concept in salutogenesis is resistance resources. These are factors that help people cope with stress and stressful situations. These include adaptive coping strategies, the ability to self-regulate, and the availability of social support.

Health-promoting lifestyle:

- Salutogenesis highlights the importance of a health-promoting lifestyle. These include eating a balanced diet, regular physical activity, getting enough sleep, and other behaviors that help promote health.

Participation and empowerment:

- Salutogenesis emphasizes the active participation of individuals in their own health process. Empowerment, i.e. the strengthening of self-efficacy and self-determination, is considered crucial for the development of health.

Holistic approach:

- Salutogenesis promotes a holistic approach to health that encompasses physical, psychological, social, and spiritual dimensions. It acknowledges the complexity of health and sees it as a dynamic process.

Salutogenesis has important implications for the design of health promotion measures and the development of interventions in social work. By focusing on health-promoting factors and strengthening the sense of coherence, salutogenesis helps to support positive health developments on an individual and collective level.

Self-determination

Self-determination refers to an individual's ability and right to make decisions about their own lives, pursue their own goals, and shape their own path. This concept is central to various areas of social work and is considered a fundamental human right.

Autonomy and independence:
- Self-determination involves the autonomy and independence of a person to make their own decisions. This includes the freedom to develop one's own beliefs, values and goals.

Personal Choices:
- Self-determination includes the possibility of choosing from various alternative courses of action. This refers not only to basic life decisions, but also to everyday matters.

Respect for personal choices:
- Respecting other people's personal choices and life paths is an essential part of self-determination. Even if decisions are different, they should be respected and accepted.

Inclusion and participation:
- Self-determination also means that people can actively participate in social processes. This includes participation in education, work, social activities, and other areas of life.

Accessibility:
- Accessibility is crucial for promoting self-determination. This includes not only physical accessibility, but also the breaking down of barriers on a social, cultural and institutional level.

Health Care and Self-Determination:
- In healthcare, self-determination plays an important role, especially in medical decisions. People should have the right to be informed about their medical treatment and to be actively involved in decisions about their health care.

Support and empowerment:
- Self-determination does not mean that people have to do everything on their own. It also includes the opportunity to receive support and actively participate in the process of empowerment to strengthen one's abilities.

Cultural Sensitivity:
- Cultural differences and individual life contexts should be taken into account when promoting self-determination. A respectful approach to cultural diversity is crucial.

In social work, it is a basic principle to respect and promote the self-determination of the clients. This includes creating a supportive environment that allows for freedom of choice and active participation in social life.

Self-efficacy

Self-efficacy refers to a person's belief that they are capable of performing certain actions and achieving certain goals that affect their life circumstances. Developed by Albert Bandura, this concept plays a key role in motivation, behavior, and success.

Self-motivation:
- Self-efficacy is closely linked to motivation. People with high self-efficacy are more motivated to take on challenges and actively work on achieving their goals.

Belief in one's own abilities:
- Self-efficacy involves believing in one's own abilities and the conviction that one is capable of acting successfully. It is a confidence in one's own competences.

Influence on action:
- The belief of self-efficacy has a significant influence on a person's actions. People who feel effective tend to choose more active strategies and overcome obstacles.

Taking on challenges:
- People with high self-efficacy are more likely to take on challenges and take on new tasks, even if they are complex or demanding.

Endurance in difficult situations:
- Self-efficacious individuals show greater perseverance in difficult situations. They don't give up easily and are more willing to look at setbacks as learning opportunities.

Homeostasis:
- Self-efficacy is associated with the ability to self-regulate. People who feel effective about themselves can regulate their own emotions, behaviors, and ways of thinking more effectively.

Positive thinking:
- The belief in self-efficacy promotes positive thinking. People with high self-efficacy tend to focus on their strengths and resources, even in challenging situations.

Learning behaviour:
- Self-efficacious people are more likely to learn new skills and evolve. They see learning as a process of self-empowerment.

Success orientation:
- People with high self-efficacy have a focus on success. They set realistic goals and believe that their efforts can lead to positive results.

Social Impact:
- Self-efficacy can be strengthened or impaired by social influence. Positive experiences, supportive social networks, and role models can increase self-efficacy.

Promoting self-efficacy is an important aspect in various fields, including education, work, psychotherapy, and personal development. Strategies to strengthen self-efficacy can include counseling, coaching, creating supportive learning environments, and providing positive feedback for goals achieved. People who feel self-efficacious are often better able to cope with life's challenges and achieve their goals.

Self-esteem

Self-esteem refers to the assessment and appreciation that a person has of himself. It plays a crucial role in mental health, influencing well-being, relationships, performance and overall life satisfaction.

Self-acceptance:
* Self-esteem involves the ability to accept oneself, with strengths and weaknesses. It is the basis for a positive self-image.

Self-respect:
* Self-esteem involves the appreciation of oneself and respect for oneself. This includes the recognition of one's own achievements and achievements.

Self-confidence:
* Healthy self-esteem is linked to self-confidence. People with positive self-esteem believe in their abilities and feel capable of overcoming challenges.

Self-efficacy:
* Self-esteem is closely linked to self-efficacy, believing in one's ability to influence one's life and bring about positive change.

Self-concept:
* Self-esteem influences a person's self-image, that is, the way they perceive themselves. Healthy self-esteem promotes a realistic and positive self-image.

Coping with defeats:
* People with strong self-esteem are better able to cope with defeats and failures. They do not see these events as a personal devaluation, but as an opportunity for personal development.

Satisfaction with oneself:
- Healthy self-esteem is often associated with higher life satisfaction. People who value themselves tend to have a more positive outlook on their lives.

Social Relationships:
- Self-esteem also affects the quality of social relationships. People with positive self-esteem can often build more authentic and supportive relationships.

Protection against psychological stress:
- Strong self-esteem often acts as a protective factor against psychological stress such as depression and anxiety. It strengthens psychological resistance (resilience).

Self-Care:
- People with healthy self-esteem tend to take better care of themselves and take care of their physical and mental health.

Self-esteem is not static and can change throughout life. Positive experiences, personal development, support from others, and the ability to self-reflect can help promote healthy self-esteem. Professional support, such as psychotherapy or counseling, can also help boost self-esteem, especially if it is affected by negative experiences or self-esteem issues.

Self-help

Self-help refers to the process by which people facing similar challenges or problems support each other to improve their quality of life. Self-help organizations provide space for sharing experiences, information, and emotional support.

Community and solidarity:

- Support groups create a community of people who share similar experiences. The solidarity within the group allows the members to feel understood and supported.

Information exchange:

- Support groups serve as a platform for sharing information about specific topics or challenges. This can include practical advice, best practices, and resources.

Emotional Support:

- A central aspect of self-help is emotional support. People can talk about their feelings in a trusting environment and learn that they are not alone.

Empowerment:

- Self-help promotes the empowerment of participants by encouraging them to actively work on their own solution or overcoming their challenges. The feeling of self-efficacy is strengthened.

Health promotion:

- Self-help contributes to health promotion by allowing members to actively work on their physical and mental health. The focus is often on preventive measures and the promotion of quality of life.

Use experiential knowledge:

- Self-help groups allow participants to share and use their personal experiential knowledge. This experiential knowledge can often be just as valuable as technical expertise.

Personal responsibility:

- Self-help promotes self-responsibility. Participants are encouraged to actively work on their own recovery or coping and to take responsibility for their decisions.

Accessibility:

- Self-help groups are often barrier-free and offer low-threshold access. People can join the group voluntarily and without formal obligations.

Variety of topics:

- Self-help organizations exist for a variety of issues, from health challenges to psychological distress to social concerns. As a result, a wide range of needs can be covered.

Active participation in decision-making:

- Support groups allow participants to actively participate in decisions that affect the group. This promotes democracy and shared responsibility.

Self-help makes a valuable contribution to psychosocial support and the promotion of quality of life. The idea of self-help is applicable in various areas of life and plays an important role in health promotion and social change.

Self-reflection

Self-reflection refers to the conscious process in which a person reflects on their own thoughts, feelings, experiences, actions, and values. Self-reflection is an important skill that helps to understand oneself, promote personal growth, and improve one's actions.

Awareness of one's own thoughts and feelings:
- Self-reflection begins with an awareness of one's own thoughts and feelings. This includes the ability to observe oneself and understand one's emotional reactions to different situations.

Self-criticism and self-acceptance:
- Self-reflection includes both the capacity for self-criticism and self-acceptance. It's about being honest with yourself without judging yourself and a willingness to learn from experience.

Identification of values and beliefs:
- Self-reflection helps to identify one's own values and beliefs. This makes it possible to become aware of how these values influence our thoughts and actions.

Analysis of experience:
- Through self-reflection, experiences can be analyzed to gain insights into one's own actions, decisions, and the dynamics of relationships.

Personal Growth:
- Self-reflection is a tool for personal growth. By understanding their own strengths and weaknesses, a person can work on their development in a targeted manner.

Relationship building:
- Self-reflection plays an important role in shaping relationships. By being aware of your own communication patterns, emotional reactions, and relationship dynamics, you can interact with others more effectively.

Improvement of self-regulation:
- Self-reflection contributes to the development of self-regulation. This means that you are better able to control emotions, make decisions consciously, and focus on goals.

Adaptation of behaviors:
- The ability to self-reflect makes it possible to identify behaviors that may not be conducive and make

adjustments. This can help bring about positive changes in one's behavior.

Self:

- Self-reflection contributes to the development of a deeper self-understanding. This includes the recognition of one's own motivations, needs and goals.

Development of empathy:

- By reflecting on one's own experiences and emotions, empathy for the experiences of others can be developed, which strengthens interpersonal communication.

The ability to self-reflect is beneficial in many professional and personal contexts, including social work, professional development, and personal relationships. It allows for a more conscious life and a deeper connection to oneself and to others.

Setting

The term "setting" generally refers to the context or framework in which an action, activity, or event takes place. In social work and psychology, the term "setting" is often used to describe the environment or context in which professional interventions, therapies, or social services take place.

Therapeutic setting:

- The therapeutic setting refers to the place and conditions under which psychotherapeutic or counselling interventions take place. This can be a practice, a clinic, or any other place designed to provide a safe space for therapeutic conversations.

School setting:

- The school setting includes the environment in which school activities take place. This includes classrooms, school buildings, playgrounds, and other areas relevant to educational activities.

Workplace setting:

- The workplace setting describes the location and conditions in the workplace. In social work, this can also refer to settings in companies or organizations where social services or programs are implemented.

Healthcare Setting:

- In healthcare, the setting includes the environment of hospitals, clinics, doctors' surgeries, or other healthcare facilities where medical or therapeutic care takes place.

Family or Family System Setting:

- The family setting refers to the home environment where family interactions and relationships take place. In therapy, the family system setting can also be considered in order to understand the dynamics within a family.

Community Setting:

- The community setting refers to the context of a community, including social, cultural, and economic elements. In social work, the community setting plays an important role in the development of programs and services for the community.

Group setting:

- Group settings refer to the context in which group activities or group therapy take place. This can be a breakout room in an institution or a specially designated place.

Online Setting:

- With increasing digitalization, online settings are also becoming more relevant. Here, interventions, consultations or therapy sessions take place virtually via the Internet.

Emergency or Crisis Intervention Setting:

- In emergency situations or crisis intervention settings, special measures are taken to support people in acute emotional or psychological emergencies. This can take place in clinics, hotlines or other facilities.

Residential setting:

- The residential setting refers to a person's place of residence, whether in their own apartment, a dormitory or another form of housing. In social work, the residential setting is important in order to understand the living conditions and needs of the clients.

Consideration of the environment is crucial to effectively adapt interventions and services and ensure that they meet people's needs in their specific context.

Severe disability

The term "severe disability" refers to a legal status that exists in many countries and affects people with significant health impairments.

Definition:

- A severe disability occurs when a person's participation in social life is significantly restricted due to physical, mental or emotional impairments. The exact definition may vary by country.

Legal basis:

- In many countries, there are laws and regulations that regulate the status of severe disability. These laws set out the criteria that must be met in order to be recognized as severely disabled and grant specific rights and benefits.

Determination of severe disability:

- The determination of severe disability is often carried out by specialized doctors or experts. In many countries, official recognition is required in order to benefit from the rights and benefits.

Rights and Benefits:

- People with severe disabilities have certain rights and benefits in many countries. These include, for example, tax relief, financial aid, access to barrier-free housing, special leave, protection against dismissal, free travel of an accompanying person on public transport and other support services.

Workplace and Integration:

- In many countries, there are regulations aimed at integrating people with severe disabilities into the labour market. This may include the creation of accessible workplaces, workplace adaptations, and other measures.

Inclusion and accessibility:

- The status of severe disability is often associated with the goal of inclusion and accessibility. Societies should be designed in such a way that people with disabilities can participate in social life as equally as possible.

Degree of disability:

- In many countries, the degree of disability is expressed as a percentage. This degree is used to quantify the severity of the disability and is often decisive for the granting of rights and benefits.

The exact regulations and definitions of severe disability may vary. It is advisable to research the specific laws and regulations of each country in order to gain an accurate understanding of the rights and support options available to people with a severe disability.

Social capital

Social capital refers to the resources, opportunities, and benefits that arise from social networks, social relationships, and social bonds. It is a concept that emphasizes how social structures and relationships can have a positive impact on the individual and the community.

Social networks:
- Social capital is closely linked to social networks. It refers to the quality and quantity of relationships a person has with other people, groups, or institutions.

Trust and Cooperation:
- Trust and cooperation are central elements of social capital. When there is a high level of trust in a community or society, it can lead to improved collaboration and cooperation.

Norms and values:
- Shared norms and values within a group or community can strengthen social capital. Sharing values fosters understanding and collaboration between people.

Participation and commitment:
- Social capital is strengthened through active participation and engagement in social activities and groups. This can refer to non-profit organizations, civic groups, sports clubs, and other groups.

Social Trust:
- Social trust is a crucial component of social capital. People who have confidence in their fellow human beings and social institutions tend to enjoy higher levels of social capital.

Information exchange:
- Social capital facilitates the exchange of information and resources within a social network. This can help improve

access to education, employment opportunities, and other important resources.

Social support:

- The presence of strong social capital often means increased social support. In times of need, people can count on their social networks for emotional, financial or practical support.

Community bonding:

- Social capital strengthens bonds within a community. People feel more connected to their community when they are involved in social networks, which can have a positive impact on community life.

Institutional Social Capital:

- In addition to individual social capital, there is also institutional social capital, which refers to the quality of relationships and cooperation between different organizations, institutions, and groups.

Economic development:

- Social capital can also have an impact on economic development. Communities with high levels of social capital tend to encourage economic activity and innovation.

Strengthening social capital in a community or society can bring a number of benefits, including better health, greater well-being, better education, and greater social inclusion. Therefore, fostering social capital is often seen as an important strategy for developing communities and improving overall well-being.

Social construction

Social construction refers to the process by which social realities, meanings, and categories are collectively created and shared. It is a social and cultural process in which people create meanings and realities together.

Construction of reality:
- Social construction concerns the construction of reality itself. This means that certain phenomena, ideas, or categories in a society are not seen as objective, predetermined reality, but as products of social agreements and interpretations.

Language and symbols:
- Language and symbols play a crucial role in social construction. Through the use of terms, language, and symbolic actions, people convey meanings and create shared understandings.

Cultural influences:
- Cultural norms, values, and beliefs have a significant influence on social construction. Different cultures can have different meanings and concepts for the same phenomenon.

Gender and Identity:
- Gender and identity are common examples of socially constructed concepts. Gender roles, gender identity, and other aspects of personal identity are not only biologically determined, but also shaped by social norms and expectations.

Institutions and Power:
- Institutions and power structures play a role in social construction. Powerful groups in society often have an

influence on which ideas are considered legitimate and acceptable.

Normality and deviation:
- The notions of normality and deviation are socially constructed. What is considered normal or deviant depends on the social, cultural and historical contexts.

Racism and Ethnicity:
- Racism and ethnic categories are socially constructed. Racial classifications and ethnic identities are shaped by social conventions and historical processes.

Societal expectations:
- Societal expectations and norms influence the social construction of behavior, relationships, and social categories. People often adapt their behavior to meet societal expectations.

Social problems:
- Social problems, such as poverty, crime, or health problems, are often results of social construction. The way these problems are defined influences the way they are perceived and addressed in society.

Discourses and Narratives:
- Discourses and narratives are means of social construction. The way certain topics are talked about influences the construction of meanings and realities.

The emphasis on social construction emphasizes that realities, identities, and meanings are not objective or natural, but the result of social processes and interactions. This concept has far-reaching implications in fields such as sociology, anthropology, psychology, and gender studies, as it helps to understand the diversity of human experiences and perspectives.

Social Gerontology

Social gerontology is a branch of gerontology that deals with the social, psychological, and societal aspects of aging. It investigates how older people live in society, what social conditions influence their well-being, and how social services can meet the needs of older people. Social gerontology deals with the following aspects

Social Change and Demographic Change:
- Social gerontology is concerned with social change in the context of demographic change, in particular the impact of an ageing population on family structures, labour markets and social systems.

Social support systems:
- One focus is on the study of social support systems for older people. These include family relationships, community networks, volunteering, and formal services.

Images of age and stereotypes:
- Social gerontology analyzes images of age and stereotypes in society and their effects on the self-image of older people as well as on the way they are perceived and treated by others.

Loneliness and social isolation:
- Loneliness and social isolation are important topics in social gerontology. The discipline investigates the causes and consequences of loneliness in the elderly and develops interventions for prevention and support.

Ageism:
- Social gerontology deals with ageism and advocates for an age-friendly society that protects the rights and resources of older people.

Care and support:
- Social gerontology studies different models of care and support for the elderly, both in family and institutional contexts. The focus is on the question of how the needs of older people can be adequately taken into account.

Health and well-being in old age:
- Health aspects, including physical and mental health, play a huge role in social gerontology. She investigates how social factors influence the well-being of older people.

Age policy:
- Social gerontology analyzes aging policies and programs to ensure they meet the needs of older people. This includes promoting inclusion, participation and social justice.

Participation and commitment in old age:
- The participation of older people in social, cultural and political activities is an important focus. Social gerontology investigates how older people can be actively integrated into society.

Ethics in dealing with the elderly:
- Ethics plays a crucial role in social gerontology, especially in dealing with vulnerable older people. The discipline looks at issues of autonomy, dignity and ethical duties towards the elderly.

Social gerontology contributes to a better understanding of the social aspects of ageing and addresses the question of how society can better support older people so that they can lead dignified and fulfilling lives.

Social group work

Social group work is a method of social work that aims to support and empower people in groups and to promote their social skills. The method is based on the idea that groups provide a unique social context in which members can learn from each other, receive support, and develop social relationships.

Teaming:
- The process begins with the formation of a group of people with similar needs, interests, or challenges. The group members can belong to different ages, backgrounds or life situations.

Objective:
- Clear goals are set for group work. These goals can be individual development goals, improving social skills, tackling specific problems, or fostering community and cohesion.

Group dynamics:
- The interactions within the group, also known as group dynamics, are of central importance. Social group work aims to foster positive group dynamics that create a supportive and nurturing environment.

Social Learning:
- The group members learn from each other through the exchange of experiences, perspectives and solutions. Social learning within the group contributes to personal development and the expansion of social skills.

Self-help and support:
- Social group work promotes the approach of self-help. Group members encourage each other, share resources, and provide emotional support in a safe environment.

Executive committee:

- A qualified group leader, often a social worker or other subject matter expert, plays a crucial role. The group leader supports the group process, promotes communication and contributes to the achievement of the group goals.

Participation:

- The active participation of all group members is encouraged. This includes sharing one's own experiences, contributing ideas and actively participating in group activities.

Reflection:

- Reflection is an important part of social group work. Group members are encouraged to reflect on their own progress, challenges, and experiences.

Diversity & Inclusion:

- The diversity of the group members is recognized and appreciated. Social group work strives for inclusion to ensure that all members are heard and respected.

Interventions and activities:

- Various interventions and activities are used to achieve the group goals. These can be creative expressions, role-playing, discussions, group exercises, and other interactive methods.

Focus on change:

- The group work is geared towards change and positive development. Group members are encouraged to develop new perspectives and find strategies for overcoming challenges.

Sustainability:

- The sustainability of group work is sought through the promotion of long-term social relationships and the establishment of supportive networks within the group.

Social group work can be used in a variety of contexts, including schools, communities, health facilities, and rehabilitative programs. It offers an effective method to promote social support, learning and personal development in a collective framework.

Social indicators

Social indicators are quantitative measures used to analyze, evaluate, and compare social phenomena. These indicators provide insights into various aspects of social life and allow researchers, decision-makers and social workers to assess social progress, prosperity, inequality and other social dimensions.

Poverty and income distribution:
- Indicators such as the level of poverty, the Gini coefficient and the median of income make it possible to assess the distribution of income and the poverty rate in a society.

Level of education:
- Education indicators include things like literacy levels, the proportion of the population with tertiary education, and participation rates at different levels of education.

Health and life expectancy:
- Social indicators in the health sector may include life expectancy, infant mortality, availability of health services and access to clean water.

Employment and working conditions:
- Indicators in this area take into account the unemployment rate, the employment rate, the proportion of precarious jobs and other factors influencing working conditions.

Housing:

- Social indicators in the housing sector cover aspects such as the proportion of the population without adequate housing, the burden of housing costs and access to basic housing conditions.

Social inequality:

- Social inequality indicators may include the Gini coefficient, the Palma index, and other measures to assess the distribution of resources in a society.

Participation and political involvement:

- Social indicators in the field of political participation measure voter turnout, membership in political organisations and levels of participation in political processes.

Crime rates:

- Crime indicators capture various forms of crime, including the rate of violent crime, property crimes, and other criminal activities.

Social capital formation:

- Social capital formation indicators can measure participation in voluntary work, membership in social groups, and social inclusion.

Environmental quality:

- Social indicators in the environmental field take into account factors such as air and water quality, access to green spaces and environmental impacts on health.

Social indicators serve as tools for monitoring, evaluating and planning social and policy measures. They make it possible to identify trends in the social field, identify inequalities and evaluate the effectiveness of interventions. Social workers and researchers use these indicators to improve the well-being of communities and develop targeted interventions.

Social Justice

Social justice is a central concept in social work and refers to the equitable distribution of resources, opportunities and rights in society.

Equality and equality:
- Social justice strives for equality and equality. This means that all people should have equal opportunities and rights regardless of their origin, gender, race, religion or other characteristics.

Combating discrimination:
- Social justice is committed to combating discrimination and fighting prejudice that leads to inequalities. This includes measures to remove structural barriers and prejudices.

Equal opportunity:
- The concept of social justice emphasizes the need for equal opportunities. All people should have equal access to education, employment, health care and other basic resources.

Distributive justice:
- Distributive justice refers to the fair distribution of resources in society. Social justice strives for a distribution that takes into account people's needs and minimizes social inequalities.

Economic Justice:
- Social justice also includes economic justice. This means tackling poverty, social exclusion and economic inequality, and creating mechanisms that enable a fair distribution of wealth.

Access to resources:
- Social justice calls for unfettered access to basic resources such as education, health care, housing, and social services for all members of society.

Participation and co-determination:

- Social justice promotes the active participation and co-determination of all people in social decision-making processes. This includes the inclusion of minority groups and disadvantaged communities.

Intersectionality:

- The concept of intersectionality is closely linked to social justice. It takes into account the interactions of different social identities and recognizes that discrimination based on gender, race, class, and other factors can be intertwined.

Human rights:

- Social justice is based on the respect and promotion of human rights. It is committed to safeguarding the dignity and rights of every individual.

Social Activism and Advocacy:

- To promote social justice, social activism and advocacy are crucial. This includes advocating for change at the political, social, and economic levels to eliminate injustices.

Social justice is a fundamental principle of social work and forms the basis for interventions, programs and policy efforts to create a more equitable and inclusive society. Social workers play a critical role in promoting social justice by tackling inequalities and addressing the needs of disadvantaged groups.

Social Labour Law

Social work law encompasses the legal framework for the practice of social work. It sets standards for the protection of clients' rights and well-being, as well as for the professional responsibility of social workers.

Data protection and confidentiality:
- Social labour law lays down rules for data protection and confidentiality of information. Social workers are required to respect the privacy of their clients and ensure that personal information is protected.

Informed Consent:
- The concept of informed consent is important in social employment law. Clients must be informed about the nature of the services, the risks and benefits, and must give their consent voluntarily and informedly.

Rights of minors:
- Social work law contains specific provisions to protect the rights of minors. This includes issues such as protection against abuse, neglect or exploitation, as well as the participation of children in decisions that affect their welfare.

Anti-discrimination and equality:
- Laws against discrimination and for equality are enshrined in social work law. Social workers have a duty to fight against all forms of discrimination and to promote equal opportunities.

Obligation to report and child protection:
- In many jurisdictions, social workers have a duty to report suspected child abuse or neglect. Social work law specifies how and when such reports must be made in order to protect the best interests of the child.

Ethics Guidelines:
- Ethics guidelines are an integral part of social work law. These guidelines provide guidelines for professional conduct, integrity, and ethical standards that must be adhered to by social workers.

Professional Licensing and Certification:
- Social work law often regulates the licensing and certification of social workers. It specifies the qualifications and requirements required to practice the profession.

Liability and risk management:
- Liability issues and risk management are important in social employment law. Social workers need to be aware of how their actions may have legal consequences and protect themselves against potential risks.

Health & Safety Regulations:
- Social work law also includes provisions on health and safety at work. This concerns both the safety of social workers and the safety of clients when services are provided directly.

Social policy and social benefits:
- Legal regulations in the field of social policy and social benefits also fall under social work law. Social workers need to learn about government support programs, social security, and other relevant legislation.

Social work law provides the legal framework that ensures that social work is carried out ethically and in accordance with the rights and needs of clients. It is important for social workers to inform themselves about the applicable laws and regulations and to observe them in their practice.

Social legislation

Social law is an area of law that deals with the legal regulations in the field of social security, social welfare and social benefits. The aim of social law is to provide protection and support to people in different life situations. It encompasses a variety of laws and regulations that contain regulations on social benefits, social security, and social services.

Social security:
- Social security law regulates various forms of social insurance, including health insurance, pension insurance, accident insurance, unemployment insurance, and long-term care insurance. These systems are intended to provide insured persons with protection and support in a variety of life situations.

Welfare:
- Social assistance law regulates state welfare benefits, in particular for persons who are not or not sufficiently able to earn their own living. These include, for example, basic security in old age and in the event of reduced earning capacity.

Unemployment law:
- Provisions in social law ensure the protection of employees in the event of unemployment. These include unemployment benefits, unemployment assistance and measures for professional reintegration.

Pension law:
- Pension law regulates entitlements to old-age pensions, disability pensions and survivors' pensions. It ensures that people are financially secure in old age or with health impairments.

Disability rights:
- Social law contains provisions for the protection and promotion of persons with disabilities. These include regulations on participation in social life, barrier-free access and support in working life.

Health insurance:
- Health insurance in social law ensures that insured persons have access to medical care. This includes services such as medical treatment, medication, hospitalization, and preventive measures.

Family law:
- Provisions in social law relate to financial support for families, especially children and single parents. These include, for example, child benefit and benefits for education and participation.

Care law:
- Long-term care law in social law regulates benefits and support for people in need of care and their relatives. These include care allowance, support for home care and benefits for inpatient care facilities.

Asylum and refugee law:
- Social regulations also affect the care and support of asylum seekers and refugees. This includes services such as housing, health care and social care.

Social Jurisdiction:
- Social law is closely linked to social justice. Disputes over social rights are heard by social courts that specialise in this particular area of law.

Social law is strongly influenced by state social policy and is often subject to changes and adaptations in order to respond to social developments. It plays a crucial role in securing the social safety net and promoting social justice.

Social Management

Social management refers to the planning, organization, implementation, and evaluation of social services and programs. It is a discipline of social work that deals with the effective management of organizations and resources in the social sector.

Organizational Development:
- Social management encompasses the development and strengthening of organizations in the social field. This includes the design of organizational structures, work processes and management systems.

Human resource management:
- The effective management of employees in the social sector is a central aspect of social management. This includes recruiting, training, motivating and evaluating employees.

Financial management:
- Financial management in the social sector refers to the management of financial resources, budgeting, and ensuring the financial sustainability of social organizations.

Quality:
- Social management attaches great importance to safeguarding and improving the quality of social services. This includes the development of quality standards, audits and improvement measures.

Strategic Management:
- Strategic management in the social field involves the development of long-term goals, plans, and strategies to achieve the mission and vision of a social organization.

Project management:

- Social management also includes effective project management. This includes the planning, implementation and monitoring of projects in the social sector.

Cooperation and networking:

- Social management emphasizes collaboration and networking with other organizations, institutions, and stakeholders. Creating partnerships helps pool resources and maximize the impact of social programs.

Evaluation and impact measurement:

- The evaluation of programmes and services is an important part of social management. Measuring the impact of social interventions helps to assess effectiveness and make necessary adjustments.

Ethics and Values:

- Social management takes into account ethical principles and values that are central to working in the social sector. This includes considering the rights and dignity of clients, employees and communities.

Politics and Advocacy:

- Social management also includes political aspects, including advocacy and advocacy. Social managers advocate for policy changes that promote the well-being of people in the social sphere.

Social management plays a critical role in the effective and efficient management of social organizations to meet the needs and challenges of the communities they serve. It integrates management, leadership, planning, and social work skills to provide a holistic approach to improving social conditions.

Social Networking

Social networking in social work refers to the use and promotion of social networks to improve the well-being and quality of life of clients.

Network Assessment:
- Social workers conduct network assessments to understand clients' existing social support systems. This includes identifying family members, friends, community resources, and other potential supporters.

Resource Mobilization:
- The aim of social networking is to mobilise resources. This involves identifying strengths and potentials in the client's social network to ensure comprehensive support.

Network Intervention:
- Social workers intervene based on network analysis to promote positive change. This can include activating support people, coordinating services, and strengthening relationships within the social network.

Social capital formation:
- Social networking aims to build social capital. This refers to the resources that result from relationships and networks, such as trust, collaboration, and support.

Family work:
- In social networking, cooperation with families plays a central role. Social workers support families in strengthening their internal relationships and in tapping into external support.

Empowerment:
- Social networking fosters client empowerment by strengthening their ability to use resources in their social network and bring about positive change.

Cultural Competence:

- Cultural competence is crucial in social networking. Social workers need to understand the cultural backgrounds and values of clients and their networks in order to develop effective interventions.

Collaboration and networking:

- Social networking involves collaborating with other professionals and organizations. This may include creating partnerships with community resources and coordinating services for clients.

Crisis intervention:

- In crisis situations, the support of the social network plays a decisive role. Social workers help clients mobilize support in their network to deal with crises.

Evaluation and monitoring:

- The continuous evaluation and monitoring of the social network are part of the social network work. Social workers regularly evaluate the effectiveness of the interventions and adjust their strategies to meet the needs of clients.

Social networking is a holistic approach that emphasizes the importance of social relationships and support systems. By strengthening social networks, social workers help foster the resilience and well-being of their clients.

Social participation

Social participation refers to the active involvement of the individual in different areas of society. This includes the opportunity to participate in social, political, cultural, economic and educational activities and to contribute to society. Social participation is an important principle for an inclusive and just society.

Social inclusion:
- Social participation goes hand in hand with social inclusion. It means that all people, regardless of their personal characteristics or life circumstances, are recognized and accepted as equal members of society.

Education and Knowledge:
- Access to education is crucial for social participation. Education enables not only personal development, but also participation in intellectual discourse and cultural life.

Political participation:
- The opportunity to engage in politics is a fundamental element of social participation. This includes the right to vote, participation in political discussions, involvement in citizens' initiatives and the exercise of civil rights.

Labour market integration:
- The opportunity to participate in the labour market and engage in meaningful professional activity is an important aspect of social participation. This includes equal opportunities, fair pay and professional development.

Cultural participation:
- Participation in cultural activities, whether through art, music, theatre or other forms of expression, promotes cultural participation. Access to cultural events and resources is an indicator of the diversity of society.

Health Participation:
- Access to adequate health care and the opportunity to make healthy life choices are crucial factors for health participation.

Social commitment:

- Volunteer work and social commitment are ways of social participation. Individuals can use their skills and resources to make a positive impact on their community.

Intercultural Dialogue:

- Participation in intercultural dialogues promotes understanding and appreciation of diversity. An open exchange between people from different backgrounds contributes to social harmony.

Accessibility:

- Accessibility is crucial for the participation of people with different abilities. This includes physical accessibility, accessibility of information technologies, and the design of environments for all.

Participation of minorities:

- Social participation requires the inclusion of minorities and marginalized groups. This includes measures to ensure that all voices are heard and that there are equal opportunities.

Social participation is a fundamental principle of a democratic and inclusive society. It requires the creation of conditions that allow all people to actively participate and contribute to social life. Active participation not only contributes to personal development, but also strengthens the social fabric and cohesion of a society.

Social Pedagogy

Social pedagogy is a pedagogical approach that aims to support people in their social development and to promote their individual potential. The focus is on social issues and challenges. Social pedagogy refers to the design of learning and development processes, taking into account social contexts.

Holistic approach:
- Social pedagogy takes a holistic approach that takes into account not only cognitive, but also emotional, social and physical aspects of development.

Prevention and intervention:
- An important goal of social pedagogy is the prevention of social problems as well as the intervention and support of people in difficult life situations.

Social integration:
- Social pedagogy strives to promote the social integration of individuals. This includes strengthening social skills, social responsibility and empowering people.

Participation:
- Participation, i.e. the participation and co-determination of individuals in decision-making processes, is a fundamental principle of social pedagogy.

Social Learning:
- Social pedagogy places a strong emphasis on social learning, in which individuals learn through interactions with others, develop social skills, and develop in their identity.

Inclusion:
- Inclusion is a central concern of social pedagogy. It aims to create a society in which all people can participate equally, regardless of their individual characteristics.

Relationship building:
- The relationship between educators and learners is of great importance in social pedagogy. A positive and supportive relationship is the foundation for effective learning and growth.

Crisis intervention:

- Social pedagogues are often active in crisis intervention. They support people in acute life crises and help them to deal appropriately with challenges.

Advice and support:

- Counselling and supportive measures are important instruments of social pedagogy. Social pedagogues offer help in coping with problems and promote the self-determination of the clients.

Intercultural work:

- Social pedagogy takes into account the diversity of cultural backgrounds and promotes intercultural skills. It is committed to the recognition and appreciation of cultural diversity.

Social pedagogy is applied in various contexts such as schools, youth welfare, family work, community work and social institutions. The aim is to support people in developing their potential, overcoming social challenges and actively participating in social life.

Social policy

Social policy refers to government policies and interventions aimed at promoting social justice, social security, and the well-being of citizens. It encompasses a variety of policies, laws, and programs aimed at addressing social problems and improving the quality of life of the population.

Social Justice:

- A central concern of social policy is the promotion of social justice. This includes access to resources, equal opportunities and the reduction of social inequality.

Social security systems:

- Social policy includes the establishment and maintenance of social security systems such as pensions, unemployment insurance, health insurance and social assistance in order to protect people from existential risks.

Education and health policy:

- Social policy plays a role in the design of education and health systems. Policies can aim to improve access to education and health care and reduce social inequalities in these areas.

Labor market policy:

- Social policy also includes measures to shape the labour market in order to ensure fair working conditions, decent wages and the protection of workers' rights.

Housing policy:

- The provision of affordable housing and measures to prevent homelessness are important aspects of social policy.

Family and youth policy:

- Social policy can focus on supporting families through parental leave, financial benefits, and childcare. Youth policy may include programmes to promote youth employment and education.

Integration of minorities:

- Promoting the integration of minorities and combating discrimination are important objectives of social policy.

Disability:

- Measures to support people with disabilities, including barrier-free access and financial support, are part of social policy.

Policy on the elderly:
- Social policy aims to address the needs of older people, including pensions, care services and age-appropriate housing.

Social investment:
- The idea of social investment emphasizes long-term investment in education, health, and social services as a means of promoting individual development and societal progress.

Social policy is influenced by political, economic and cultural factors. However, the goal is always to create a just and inclusive society where the basic needs of citizens are met and everyone has the opportunity to reach their full potential.

Social Psychiatric Service

The Social Psychiatric Service is an institution of psychiatry and social work that deals with the support and accompaniment of people with mental illnesses. He often works in an interdisciplinary manner and offers a variety of services to improve the quality of life and social integration of people with mental health problems.

Advice and support:
- The Social Psychiatric Service provides counselling services for people with mental health problems and their relatives.

This can include help in coping with challenges in everyday life, social integration and the development of individual coping strategies.

Social integration:

- One focus is on promoting the social integration of people with mental illnesses. This may include assistance in finding suitable housing, jobs, and social activities.

Crisis intervention:

- The Social Psychiatric Service often provides crisis intervention services. This includes supporting people in acute crisis situations to avoid inpatient psychiatric admission if this is possible and reasonable.

Cooperation with other institutions:

- The service works closely with other mental health facilities, health services, social services, support groups, and community-based organizations to ensure comprehensive care.

Prevention and education:

- The Social Psychiatric Service is often involved in preventive measures and mental health education. This may include training, information sessions, and promoting mental health in the community.

Help with applications:

- People with mental illness often need assistance in applying for benefits and support. The Social Psychiatric Service offers assistance in applying for social benefits, pensions, housing assistance and other relevant benefits.

Outpatient care:

- An important aspect of the social psychiatric service is outpatient care. This means that support is offered directly in the living environment of the person concerned in order to ensure the highest possible quality of life.

Promoting self-determination:

- The service promotes self-determination and autonomy for people with mental illnesses. This includes involving data subjects in decisions about their treatment and support.
Aftercare:
- After psychiatric stays or other intensive interventions, the Social Psychiatric Service often provides follow-up services to ensure stable and ongoing support.

The Social Psychiatric Service plays a crucial role in creating an inclusive and supportive environment for people with mental illness.

Social security

Social security is a system of government policies aimed at ensuring the economic security and well-being of citizens. This security is achieved through the provision of financial benefits and support in certain life situations.

Health insurance:
- Health insurance is an essential part of social security. It covers the costs of medical treatment, medicines, hospitalization, and other health services.
Pension scheme:
- Pension insurance offers financial security in old age. Employees pay into the scheme during their working life and receive regular pension payments in retirement.

Unemployment insurance:

- Unemployment insurance protects employees from financial losses in the event of unemployment. It grants unemployment benefit as an income replacement benefit for a certain period of time.

Accident insurance:

- Accident insurance provides protection and financial benefits in the event of accidents at work or work-related illnesses. This includes medical treatment, rehabilitation and, if applicable, pension payments.

Long-term care insurance:

- Long-term care insurance supports people who are dependent on help due to the need for long-term care. It covers care services at home or in care facilities.

Maternity insurance:

- Maternity insurance provides financial benefits during pregnancy and after childbirth. This may include maternity pay and additional support.

Family insurance:

- Family insurance provides financial benefits for families with children. These include child benefit, family-related benefits and assistance with childcare costs.

Disability insurance:

- Disability insurance provides financial support for people who are permanently unable to work due to disability. This includes pension payments and rehabilitation.

Benefits in the event of death:

- Social Security provides death benefits to provide financial support to surviving dependents. This may include widow's/widower's pension, orphan's pension, and funeral expenses.

Contribution financing:

- Social security is often funded by contributions paid by employers, employees, and in some cases, the state. These contributions form the financing pool for the various services.

Principle of solidarity:

- Many social security systems are based on the principle of solidarity. This means that those who pay into the system receive benefits for those who need them, regardless of individual income or health differences.

Legal basis:

- Social security is based on laws and regulations. These set out the conditions for access to benefits, contribution rates and other relevant aspects.

Social security plays a central role in safeguarding the social safety net and supporting citizens in various life situations. Its goal is to promote economic stability and the well-being of the population.

Social services

The term "social service" can have different meanings in different contexts. Here are some possible interpretations, depending on the context:

Hospital Social Services:

- The hospital social service operates in medical facilities and provides social support and counseling to patients and their families. This may include help with social, financial, or emotional issues related to an illness or medical treatment.

General Social Service at the Social Welfare Office:

- In many countries, the General Social Service exists as part of the Social Welfare Office or Youth Welfare Office. This institution offers general social services, including financial support, counselling on social issues, support in coping with life crises and protection measures for children and young people.

Social service in companies:

- Some larger companies have a company social service. This supports employees in their personal and professional challenges. Services can range from counselling services to the provision of support services.

Social Service in Schools:

- School social workers or social pedagogues in schools provide support to students and their families with academic, social and personal challenges. This can include counselling, prevention work, conflict resolution and support for school transitions.

Social service in geriatric care:

- In care facilities for the elderly, there are often social services that provide social support to residents and their families. This may include help in adapting to the life situation in the institution, psychosocial support and arranging support services.

Social service in the care of the disabled:

- Disability care facilities have social services that provide support to people with disabilities and their families. This can include advice on the selection of suitable support services, promotion of participation and support in legal matters.

Social Space Analysis

Social space analysis is a methodological approach in social work that aims to gain a comprehensive insight into the social, cultural, economic and structural conditions of a given geographical area. It forms the basis for the development of targeted interventions and measures to improve living conditions in this area.

Geographical demarcation:
- The social space analysis begins with the clear definition and delimitation of the geographical area to be studied, be it a neighborhood, a neighborhood or a rural community.

Data collection:
- The analysis involves the systematic collection of data, both quantitative and qualitative. Various methods such as surveys, observations, statistical evaluations and expert interviews can be used.

Social Structures:
- The social structures in the study area are analyzed, including age structure, ethnic composition, family structures, and social classes.

Economic aspects:
- The economic conditions, job opportunities, income distribution and unemployment rate in the social area are examined.

Infrastructure:
- The availability and quality of infrastructure, including educational institutions, health services, transport links, leisure facilities and housing, will be analysed.

Social networks:
- The study of social networks and community structures plays an important role. This includes social relationships, group activities, and the degree of social integration.

Health:
- Health-related indicators such as disease rates, access to health services and life expectancy can be included in the analysis.

Level of education:
- The level of education of the residents, school quality and access to further education opportunities are important aspects in the social space analysis.

Cultural factors:
- Cultural factors such as shared values, traditions and cultural institutions are taken into account.

Participation and involvement:
- The analysis evaluates the existing forms of participation and participation of residents in decision-making processes in the social space.

Problem Identification:
- Social space analysis helps to identify social problems and challenges that exist in the study area.

Stakeholder analysis:
- The interests and resources of the various actors and organisations in the social area, including residents, local businesses, associations and administrations, are analysed.

The results of a social space analysis serve as a basis for the development of needs-based and targeted measures and interventions in social work. The participatory nature of this analysis makes it possible to adequately take into account the perspectives and needs of the residents and to promote sustainable positive change in the social space.

Social space design

Social space design is an active process in which the results of social space analysis and diagnosis are translated into concrete actions to improve the quality of life and well-being in a given geographical area. This approach to social work emphasizes participatory collaboration with the community and other actors.

Participation and involvement:
- The residents of the social space are actively involved in the design process. Their perspectives, needs and ideas play a central role in the development of measures.

Community work:
- Social space design involves community outreach, where social workers, community workers, and other professionals work directly with the community to identify needs and develop solutions.

Development of resources:
- The design of the social space aims to strengthen existing resources and develop new ones. These can be individual skills as well as institutional support and infrastructure.

Interventions and projects:
- Based on the results of the social space analysis, concrete interventions and projects will be developed. These can be educational programs, health initiatives, employment projects, or other measures aimed at the identified needs.

Creation of meeting spaces:
- The creation of meeting spaces and places where the community can come together promotes social cohesion and strengthens social networks in the social space.

Cultural and social events:

- The organization of cultural and social events helps to strengthen the identity and sense of community in the social space.

Education:

- Education, both formal and informal, is an important part of social space design. They can increase the level of education of residents and improve access to knowledge and skills.

Infrastructure Improvements:

- Where necessary, infrastructure improvements will be made to facilitate access to essential facilities such as schools, health centres and leisure facilities.

Community Empowerment:

- Social space design strives for community empowerment, empowering people to shape their own affairs and drive change in their living environment.

Sustainability and Evaluation:

- The sustainability of the measures taken is taken into account. Mechanisms for the ongoing evaluation and adaptation of interventions will be implemented.

Cooperation with local actors:

- The design of social spaces often requires cooperation with local organisations, companies, authorities and other actors. These collaborations strengthen the ability to implement and the impact of the measures.

Social space design is a dynamic and participatory process that aims to sustainably improve living conditions and opportunities in a given geographical area. By collaborating with the community and considering their needs and resources, social space design helps to create an inclusive and livable environment.

Social Space Diagnosis

The social space diagnosis is a further step in the social space analysis and refers to the evaluation and interpretation of the collected data and information. It is a social work tool to identify the specific needs, resources, potentials and challenges in a given geographical area.

Data Interpretation:
- Social space diagnosis involves the careful interpretation of the data collected. The aim is to identify patterns, trends and connections between different aspects of the social space.

Market analysis:
- The diagnosis aims to identify the specific needs of the residents in the social space. This can extend to education, health, job opportunities, housing, and other areas.

Resource Analysis:
- In addition to the identification of needs, existing resources and potentials in the social space are also analyzed. This includes individual skills, social networks, nonprofits, and other supporting structures.

Problem Identification:
- Social space diagnosis helps to identify social problems and challenges that exist in the examination room. This can include social inequality, unemployment, educational inequality, and other issues.

Residents' participation:
- Residents' involvement is a central aspect of social space diagnosis. Through participatory approaches, residents' perspectives and experiences are included in the diagnosis.

Contextual Analysis:
- The social space diagnosis takes into account the social and cultural context of the area under investigation. This is

necessary to understand the meaning and relevance of data.

Stakeholder involvement:

- The analysis involves various stakeholders, including local community members, organizations, businesses, and public institutions. Your perspectives and resources will be integrated into the diagnosis.

Preparation of recommendations for action:

- On the basis of the diagnosis, concrete recommendations for action are developed. These can range from targeted interventions to long-term development plans.

Monitoring and evaluation:

- The social space diagnosis also lays the foundation for monitoring and continuous evaluation. This makes it possible to track the progress of interventions and make adjustments as needed.

Communication of the results:

- The results of the social space diagnosis are communicated transparently and comprehensibly for the residents as well as for relevant stakeholders. This promotes acceptance and support for possible measures.

Social space diagnosis is a dynamic process that takes into account the complexity of the social space and aims to develop needs-based and effective measures to improve quality of life and equal opportunities.

Social Space Orientation

Social space orientation is a fundamental approach in social work that aims to understand and support people in their concrete social environment. The focus is not only on individual needs and problems, but also on the social, cultural and structural conditions of the living space.

Holistic approach:
- Social space orientation pursues a holistic approach that takes into account both individual and collective aspects of people's living environments.

Life-world orientation:
- The term "living environment" is at the heart of social space orientation. It is about understanding people's living conditions in the context of their everyday lives, their environment and their social relationships.

Participation and involvement:
- A central principle of social space orientation is the active participation of people in decision-making processes that affect their immediate living environment. Participation promotes self-determination and strengthens the community.

Resource orientation:
- The social space orientation places a strong focus on existing resources and potentials in a particular living space. This includes individual skills as well as community and institutional resources.

Social networks:
- The analysis and strengthening of social networks and relationships within a social space are of great importance. A supportive social environment contributes to people's well-being.

Demand orientation:

- Interventions and support are based on the identified needs of the residents in the social space. It's about developing solutions that meet your needs.

Community work:

- Community work is an essential part of social space orientation. Social workers and other professionals work directly with the community to understand their needs and work together to develop solutions.

Cultural Sensitivity:

- It is important to take cultural diversity into account in the social space. The social space orientation is based on cultural sensitivity and respect for different lifestyles and values.

Interventions at different levels:

- Social space orientation strives for interventions at different levels, be it at the individual, family, community or structural level.

Contextual Analysis:

- The contextual analysis of the social space is crucial. The social space orientation takes into account local conditions, social structures, historical developments and current challenges.

Empowerment:

- The empowerment of the residents is at the heart of the social space orientation. People should be empowered to shape their own living conditions and to participate in decision-making processes.

Sustainability:

- The social space orientation strives for sustainable change. Measures should be effective in the long term and improve the quality of life of the residents in the long term.

Social space orientation is thus a proactive approach to improving the living conditions of people in their immediate living environment. By involving residents, emphasizing resources, and taking into account the social context, social space orientation helps to bring about needs-based and sustainable change.

Social Space/Social Space Orientation

The term "social space" refers to a geographically defined space in which people live and maintain social relationships. Social space orientation is an approach in social work that aims to understand and improve people's living conditions in the context of their immediate social environment.

Defined geographical area:
- Social space refers to a physical space defined by geographical boundaries. This can be a neighborhood, a neighborhood, or a municipality.

People's living environment:
- The focus of social space orientation is on the living environment of people in a certain geographical area. This includes housing, working conditions, educational institutions, leisure opportunities and other aspects of daily life.

Participation and involvement:
- A central principle of social space orientation is the promotion of participation and participation of people in the social life of their area. The aim is to involve residents in decision-making processes and to take their interests into account.

Resources and potentials:
- Social space orientation emphasizes the identification and strengthening of existing resources and potentials in a geographical area. This includes individual skills as well as institutional and community resources.

Social networks:
- The analysis and promotion of social networks in a social space are important elements. The quality of social relationships and networks affects people's well-being.

Quality of life and well-being:
- The aim of social space orientation is to improve the quality of life and well-being of the residents. This is done through targeted measures that are tailored to the specific needs and challenges of the social space.

Social problems:
- The social space orientation also takes into account social problems that may arise in a certain geographical area. These include poverty, educational inequality, unemployment and other challenges.

Interdisciplinary cooperation:
- Social space orientation requires interdisciplinary cooperation between different actors such as social workers, educational institutions, health services and local administrations to ensure comprehensive support.

Community work:
- Community work is a central methodology of social space orientation. It involves working with the local community to jointly develop solutions to existing challenges.

Empowerment:
- By taking into account the needs, resources and potentials of the social space, the social space orientation strives for the empowerment of the residents and enables people to actively shape their living situation.

Social space orientation thus emphasizes that the living situation and needs of people in a certain geographical area must not be considered in isolation. Rather, solutions and assistance should be developed in an overall context that takes into account local conditions and resources.

Social Work in Addiction Care

Social work in addiction care focuses on supporting people with addictions and their families. The aim is to offer prevention, intervention and rehabilitation to reduce dependence and improve the quality of life of those affected.

Prevention:
- Social workers advocate for preventive measures to prevent addiction problems. This may include education, training programs, and awareness raising in schools, communities, and workplaces.

Counselling and intervention:
- Social workers provide individual or group counselling for people with addiction problems. Interventions can be crisis-oriented and aimed at coping with acute problems.

Resource Brokerage:
- Providing resources is an important aspect of addiction care. Social workers help identify appropriate therapy facilities, support groups, and other support services.

Case Management:

- Social workers often take on the role of case manager by analysing individual needs, developing support plans and ensuring coordination of services.

Family support:

- Addictions can have a significant impact on families. Social workers provide support and counseling for family members to help them deal with the effects of addiction.

Withdrawal and rehabilitation:

- Social workers work with people who are going through withdrawal or are in a rehabilitation phase. They support the development of life skills, stress management and the prevention of relapses.

Reintegration into the labour market:

- Returning to the labour market can be challenging for people with addictions. Social workers provide support for professional reintegration, including career guidance and training.

Support groups:

- The promotion and organization of self-help groups is an important part of addiction care. Social workers assist in the creation and management of groups to promote the exchange of experiences and mutual support.

Community Integration:

- Social workers promote the integration of people into the community by organizing activities and programs that support a positive, sober way of life.

Root cause analysis and prevention:

- Social workers are committed to understanding the causes of addictions and develop prevention programs that target individual, social, and environmental factors.

Social work in addiction care is holistically oriented and integrates medical, psychological, social and professional aspects. The aim is to help people with addiction problems to live a stable, addiction-free life and improve their quality of life.

Social Work in Disability Assistance

Social work in disability care focuses on supporting people with different disabilities, improving their quality of life, promoting their participation in society and strengthening their self-determination.

Individual needs analysis:
- Social workers conduct an individual needs assessment to understand the specific needs, skills, and resources of people with disabilities.

Promoting self-determination:
- Social work in disability care aims to promote the self-determination of people with disabilities. This means respecting their freedom of choice and involving them in decisions that affect their lives.

Social integration:
- Support for social integration is a key concern. Social workers promote the participation of people with disabilities in various areas of life, such as education, employment, leisure, and social activities.

Family support:
- Social workers provide support to families of people with disabilities. This can include advice, resource referral, and assistance in planning for the future.

Education and professional integration:
- Programmes to promote education and professional integration are developed to enable people with disabilities to participate in educational institutions and the labour market.

Accessibility:
- Social workers are committed to creating accessible environments, both physically and socially. This includes breaking down barriers to entry and promoting inclusive practices.

Assistance services:
- Social workers help organize assistance services that support people with disabilities in everyday life, whether it's personal care, mobility, or other activities.

Psychosocial support:
- People with disabilities may need psychosocial support, whether due to burdens caused by the disability itself or due to social challenges. Social workers offer therapeutic interventions to address these needs.

Intercultural Competence:
- Cross-cultural sensitivity is important to take into account the diversity of needs and backgrounds of people with disabilities, especially when it comes to cultural differences in the perception of disability.

Inclusive leisure and sports activities:
- Social workers promote inclusive leisure and sports activities to support the participation of people with disabilities in cultural and social activities.

The aim of social work in disability care is to break down barriers, promote equal opportunities and help people with disabilities to lead a self-determined and fulfilled life. Through targeted support, social workers help people with disabilities to develop their potential and be recognized as equal members of society.

Social Work in Health Care

Social work in health care encompasses a variety of tasks and interventions aimed at supporting the social and emotional needs of people in health care settings.

Psycho-social support:
- Healthcare social workers provide psycho-social support to patients and their families. This can include coping with disease diagnoses, providing support with emotional challenges, and promoting mental health.

Crisis intervention:
- Social workers play an important role in crisis intervention. They support people facing acute physical or mental health crises and help develop coping strategies.

Consultation:
- Counselling is a central part of social work in the health sector. Social workers provide individual or family counseling to help patients process disease diagnoses, make decisions about medical treatments, and cope with life changes.

Resource Brokerage:
- Social workers help identify and make resources accessible to patients. This may include financial assistance, accommodation, rehabilitation services, and other supportive services.

Coordination of care:
- Social workers often play a coordinating role in the interdisciplinary care team. They foster collaboration between different healthcare providers to ensure that patients' needs are met in a comprehensive and coordinated manner.

Palliative and hospice care:

- Healthcare social workers support patients and their families in palliative and hospice-related situations. This includes promoting quality of life, emotional support, and end-of-life planning.

Ethics advice:

- Social workers are often involved in ethics counseling, especially when it comes to difficult health care decisions. They support patients, families and medical staff in ethical considerations and decisions.

Health promotion and prevention:

- Social workers are involved in health promotion and prevention activities. This may include educating people about health risks, promoting healthy lifestyles, and helping prevent disease.

Patient Advocacy:

- Social workers act as advocates for patients' needs and rights. They help ensure that patients receive appropriate care and resources, and that their wishes and preferences are taken into account.

Cultural Sensitivity:

- Healthcare social workers take into account cultural differences and sensitivities to ensure that care and support meet the individual needs of patients.

Social work in healthcare plays a crucial role in addressing the complex social, emotional, and practical challenges associated with health problems. The support of social workers helps to improve patients' quality of life and promote a holistic approach to health care.

Social Work in Psychosocial Care

Social work in mental health care includes various interventions and support measures to help people with mental health problems and their families. This form of social work aims to promote well-being, mental health and social inclusion.

Psychosocial counselling:
- Social workers provide psychosocial counseling for individuals and groups to assist in coping with mental health issues, relationship problems, and life crises.

Crisis intervention:
- Crisis intervention is an important part of psychosocial care. Social workers help people in acute crisis situations, offer emotional support and, if necessary, arrange further professional help.

Case Management:
- Social workers often take on the role of case manager by analysing the needs of individuals with mental health issues, developing individualised support plans, and ensuring coordination of services.

Family support:
- Mental health issues can greatly affect family life. Social workers provide support to family members of people with mental illness to help them deal with the situation and strengthen family support.

Rehabilitation planning:
- Social workers assist in the development of rehabilitation plans aimed at promoting the skills and self-management of people with mental health problems.

Social integration:
- Social work in psychosocial care promotes the social integration of people with mental health problems, whether

through participation in social activities or reintegration into the labour market.

Assistance with medication intake:

- Especially for people taking medication to treat mental illness, social workers provide support and information on how to take medication, often working closely with other health care providers.

Promoting quality of life:

- Social workers promote the quality of life of people with mental health problems by identifying their personal goals, strengthening their resources, and helping them live fulfilling lives.

Development of self-help groups:

- Social workers can organize and promote support groups to bring people with similar experiences together, facilitate the exchange of information and support.

Prevention of stigma:

- Social workers advocate for the prevention of stigma related to mental health problems in order to promote understanding in society and reduce prejudice.

Social work in mental health care aims to identify individual needs, strengthen resources, and provide comprehensive support to improve the quality of life of people with mental health problems. This can be achieved through a combination of therapeutic, counselling, and practical interventions.

Social Work in Schools

School social work aims to support students and their families in various areas of life. The main objectives are to promote emotional and social development, to overcome academic and personal challenges, and to create a positive learning environment.

School intervention:
- Social workers offer school-based interventions to support students with academic challenges, whether through tutoring, behavior management, or special support programs.

Individual advice:
- A central aspect of social work in schools is the individual counselling of pupils. This can include topics such as personal development, social relationships, academic performance, and future planning.

Family support:
- Social workers provide support for families to encourage positive collaboration between school and family. This can include parent counseling, family conflict resolution, and support in coping with family challenges.

Prevention of early school leaving:
- Social workers work to prevent early school leaving by supporting students who are at risk. This includes the identification of risk factors and the development of measures to maintain school participation.

Conflict Resolution and Mediation:
- Social workers promote conflict resolution skills and provide mediation services to facilitate the management of conflict between students, teachers, or within groups.

Behavioral Management:

- Social workers work on behavioral management strategies to help students with behavioral problems or disciplinary challenges. This can include individualized care and the development of behavioral plans.

Anti-bullying programs:

- Social workers are involved in the development and implementation of anti-bullying programs to promote a safe and supportive school climate.

Health promotion:

- Health promotion is an important aspect of social work in schools. This can include promoting healthy lifestyles, mental health education, and support for health problems.

Mediation of extracurricular resources:

- Social workers connect schools with extracurricular resources and services that meet students' needs, whether through nonprofits, therapists, or other support services.

Career guidance and future planning:

- Social workers support students in career guidance and planning for their future. This includes the promotion of education and professional development.

School social work contributes to the creation of a comprehensive support structure for students. By collaborating with teachers, parents, and other professionals in the school environment, social workers help create a positive and nurturing learning environment.

Social work in the field of refugee aid

Social work in refugee aid is a special form of social work that aims to support and integrate people who have left their home country due to conflict, persecution or natural disasters. This form of social work requires a holistic and culturally sensitive approach.

Basic Needs and Emergency Care:
- Emergency assistance includes securing basic needs such as shelter, food, water, clothing and medical care for newly arriving refugees.

Psychosocial support:
- Refugees have often had traumatic experiences due to war, displacement or other stressful circumstances. Social work in the field of refugee aid includes psychosocial support to cope with trauma and promote mental health.

Social integration:
- Social work strives for the social integration of refugees in order to promote their participation in society. This can include support in learning the local language, cultural orientation and teaching basics about the new living environment.

Education and Vocational Integration:
- Support for education and professional integration is crucial. This includes access to educational institutions, skills training and job search support.

Legal advice and support:
- Social workers in the field of refugee assistance often provide legal support to help refugees clarify their status, asylum applications, and other legal matters.

Family reunification:
- Social work assists in the reunification of separated family members and offers help with bureaucratic procedures and applications.

Networking with local resources:
- Social workers build bridges with local communities, resources, and organizations to facilitate refugee integration and reduce prejudice.

Child and youth work:
- Particular attention is paid to supporting children and young people in order to promote their school integration, psychosocial development and trauma management.

Intercultural Competence:
- Social work in the field of refugee aid requires intercultural competence to ensure cultural sensitivity and understanding of the different needs of refugees.

Empowerment and participation:
- Social workers promote the empowerment of refugees by strengthening their self-determination and participation in the decision-making process. This can be done through training, participatory projects and the promotion of self-help initiatives.

Social work in refugee aid is demanding and requires a comprehensive understanding of individual needs, cultural backgrounds and political frameworks. The focus is on supporting the refugees in building a new life and integrating into their new environment.

Social Work in the Penitentiary System

Prison social work is a specialised form of social work that aims to support prisoners during their time in prison, strengthen their social skills, promote their rehabilitation and facilitate their reintegration into society after release. Social work in the prison system includes the following main areas:

Rehabilitation:
- One of the main goals of social work in the prison system is the rehabilitation of prisoners. Social workers develop programs and interventions to prepare inmates for life outside of prison and improve their chances of successful reintegration.

Individual assessments:
- Social workers conduct individual assessments to understand each inmate's needs, abilities, and challenges. This forms the basis for tailor-made intervention plans.

Therapeutic interventions:
- Social workers provide therapeutic support to help inmates cope with mental health issues, addiction issues, and other emotional challenges.

Education and professional development:
- Education and professional development programs are developed by social workers to prepare inmates for the labor market. This may include schooling, vocational training, and job coaching.

Family support:
- Social workers provide support to inmates' families to maintain relationships and create a more stable environment for inmates to return to the community.

Conflict Resolution and Anger Management:
- Social workers promote conflict resolution skills and anger management to reduce the risk of violence within the prison environment and teach inmates alternative strategies.

Legal advice:
- Social workers provide legal advice to ensure inmates understand their rights and can resolve legal issues related to their time in prison.

Preparation for dismissal:
- Social workers assist inmates in planning their discharge by identifying resources for housing, employment, and other living needs.

Addiction counselling and rehabilitation:
- Social workers offer addiction counseling and rehabilitation programs to help inmates overcome addiction problems and reduce the likelihood of relapse.

Aftercare:
- Social workers provide aftercare support after discharge to ensure that former inmates receive ongoing support in overcoming challenges related to reintegration.

Social work in the prison system plays a crucial role in preparing prisoners for successful reintegration into society and in reducing recidivism rates. Through holistic and individualized interventions, social workers help prisoners develop the necessary resources and skills to bring about positive changes in their lives.

Social Work Management

Social work management refers to the planning, organization, management, and control of social services and programs. It also includes the efficient use of resources, cooperation with various stakeholders and ensuring the quality of social services.

Programming and Development:
- Social work management involves the planning and development of programs that meet the needs of clients. This includes setting goals, strategies, and resources for the implementation of social services.

Resource Management:
- Effective resource management is crucial for the success of social services. This includes the management of funds, personnel, time and other material resources.

Personnel management and development:
- Social work managers are responsible for leading and developing their teams. This includes guiding employees, nurturing their professional development, and ensuring a positive work environment.

Quality:
- Ensuring the quality of social services is a central element of management. Social work managers develop and implement quality standards, monitor performance, and conduct evaluations.

Cooperation and networking:
- Social work management requires collaboration with various stakeholders, including government agencies, nonprofits, communities, and other service providers. Forming networks is crucial to share resources and improve the effectiveness of services.

Budgeting and financial management:
- Social work managers are responsible for creating and monitoring budgets. They must ensure that financial resources are used efficiently to achieve the goals of social services.

Politics and Advocacy:
- Social work managers play a role in the development of policies and advocacy efforts. They advocate for policies that support the needs of their clients and represent the interests of their organizations at the political level.

Information Technology and Data Management:
- The effective use of information technology and data management is important for social work management. This includes using software to manage, report, and analyze key performance indicators.

Crisis management:
- Social work managers need to be able to act in crisis situations. This includes developing contingency plans, training staff in crisis intervention, and coordinating resources in emergency situations.

Evaluation and Research:
- Continuous evaluation of programs and services is crucial. Social work managers use evaluation methods to evaluate the effectiveness of their interventions and identify potential improvements.

Social work management requires a combination of leadership skills, organizational skills, and a deep understanding of clients' needs. Through effective management, social services can be optimized and their positive impact on the community maximized.

Social Work Practice

The practice of social work refers to the application of social work theories, methods, and techniques to support and empower people in different life situations.

Casework:
- Casework is a fundamental aspect of social work practice. Social workers work individually with clients to understand their specific needs, set goals, and develop interventions to promote positive change.

Group work:
- In group work, interventions are carried out in group contexts. This may include leading support groups, social skills training, or other group activities to promote social well-being.

Teamwork:
- Social workers engage in community work to address social issues at a macro level. This may include organizing community projects, collaborating with local organizations, and developing resources for the community.

Consultation:
- Counseling is an essential part of social work practice. Social workers provide emotional support, advice, and guidance in various areas of life to address individual or family challenges.

Crisis intervention:
- Social workers are able to intervene effectively in crisis situations. This may include providing emergency assistance, coordinating resources, and assisting in coping with acute stresses.

Community Organizing:
- Community organizing involves mobilizing communities to achieve common goals. Social workers play a role in

organizing advocacy efforts and promoting social justice at the community level.

Anti-Oppression and Diversity:

- Social work practice emphasizes advocating against oppression and promoting diversity and inclusion. Social workers actively advocate against discrimination and inequality and take cultural diversity into account in their work.

Empowerment:

- Empowerment is a central principle of social work practice. Social workers empower their clients by nurturing their skills, resources, and self-determination.

Systemic work:

- Systemic work in social work practice takes into account the interactions between individual, family, social and structural factors. Social workers analyze and intervene at different levels to promote sweeping change.

Evidence-Based Practice:

- Evidence-based practice refers to the integration of research findings and best practices into social work. Social workers use evidence-based approaches to identify effective interventions and improve their practice.

Social work practice is diverse and requires a wide range of skills, including communication, empathy, critical thinking, and cultural sensitivity. Through the application of best practices and continuous reflection, social workers contribute to the well-being of individuals, families and communities.

Social Work Research

Social work research is a field that deals with the systematic study of social phenomena, interventions, practices, and challenges in social work.

Research Objectives:
- Social work research has various objectives, including improving practices, identifying best practices, solving social problems, evaluating interventions, and expanding knowledge in the field of social work.

Practical relevance:
- Research in social work is geared towards generating practice-relevant insights. This means that the research should help to improve the quality of services and better meet the needs of clients.

Participatory Research:
- Participatory research actively involves the affected persons in the research process. This fosters collaboration between researchers and clients to develop real-world insights and solutions.

Program Evaluation:
- Research in social work often involves program evaluations to evaluate the effectiveness of interventions and social programs. This can help to use resources more efficiently and promote positive change.

Empirical Methods:
- Research in social work uses a variety of empirical methods, including qualitative and quantitative approaches. These can include interviews, surveys, case studies, statistical analysis, and other techniques to collect and interpret data.

Ethics in Research:
- Research ethics plays a crucial role in social work research. This includes protecting the privacy and confidentiality of

participants, ensuring their informed consent, and ethical responsibility to the communities concerned.

Interdisciplinary cooperation:
- Research in social work often benefits from interdisciplinary collaboration. By collaborating with experts from other disciplines, new perspectives and approaches can be incorporated into research.

Social Policy and Advocacy:
- Social work research contributes to the development of social policy by providing evidence-based arguments for positive change in policy-making processes. Research results can also be used for advocacy purposes.

Community-based Research:
- Community-based research (CBR) emphasizes close collaboration with communities. This form of research actively involves the community in the research process and promotes the translation of research results into concrete actions.

Research:
- Funding research in social work is critical to providing resources for projects, scholarships, and programs that help expand and deepen knowledge in the field of social work.

Social work research is a dynamic field that helps to understand the effectiveness of interventions, identify good practice, and develop innovative approaches to social challenges. By integrating research into practice, social work is further strengthened as an evidence-based and effective discipline.

Social work with children and adolescents

Social work with children and young people aims to promote the development, well-being and social integration of young people.

Individual advice:
- Social workers provide individual counselling for children and young people to help them with personal challenges, school problems, family difficulties and other life issues.

Family support:
- Social workers work closely with families to provide support in overcoming challenges, stabilizing family life, and fostering positive relationships.

Crisis intervention:
- In crisis situations, social workers provide quick and effective support, whether in family crises, traumatic events or personal problems, to ensure the safety and well-being of children and young people.

School intervention:
- Social workers work in schools to support students with academic challenges, whether through learning support, behavior management, or coping with social issues.

Youth welfare and juvenile court assistance:
- In youth welfare and juvenile court assistance, social workers support young people who have come into conflict with the law through interventions, counselling and the development of alternatives to the penal system.

Early intervention:
- Social workers are involved in early intervention in order to identify potential risks and needs in children and

adolescents at an early stage and to provide appropriate support.

Addiction prevention and counselling:

- Social workers offer addiction prevention programs to educate children and adolescents about the risks of addictive behaviors, as well as counseling for young people with addiction problems.

Leisure and youth work:

- The organisation of leisure and youth work programmes promotes positive social activities, engagement and a sense of community among young people.

Transition to adult life:

- Social workers assist young people in their transition to adulthood by providing career guidance, help with finding training, and support in developing life skills.

Inclusion and Diversity:

- Social workers are committed to the inclusion of all children and young people, regardless of gender, ethnicity, religion or disability. They foster an environment that respects and supports diversity.

Social work with children and young people aims to create a safe, supportive and nurturing environment in which young people can develop their potential. By working with families, schools, communities and other stakeholders, social workers help to promote positive developmental trajectories for children and young people and to minimise potential risks.

Social work with homeless people

Social work with homeless people focuses on individual needs, facilitating access to basic resources, and supporting long-term stabilization.

Street Social Work:
- Social workers actively take to the streets to provide direct support to homeless people. They provide basic services such as food, clothing, and hygiene items to meet acute needs.

Emergency accommodation and accommodation search:
- Social workers help homeless people find emergency shelters, transitional housing, or long-term housing solutions. This may include coordination with accommodation facilities, landlords and other relevant stakeholders.

Health care:
- Access to health care is crucial for homeless people. Social workers assist in arranging medical care, psychological support and addiction treatment.

Livelihood:
- Social workers help homeless people meet existential needs, including financial support, access to government benefits, food, and clothing.

Social integration:
- Social work with homeless people aims to promote their social integration. This includes participating in community activities, building social networks, and reducing stigma.

Employment and education:
- Social workers help homeless people integrate into the workforce through job placement, vocational training, and skills development to improve their employability.

Addiction support and psychosocial support:

- Because many homeless people face addiction issues and mental health issues, social workers provide addiction assistance and psychosocial support.

Rehabilitation and resocialization:

- Social workers work to rehabilitate homeless people and promote their resocialization by providing support in overcoming challenges and building a stable living environment.

Legal support:

- Social workers provide legal support to help homeless people with legal issues, such as homelessness and legal rights.

Prevention of homelessness:

- An important aspect of social work with homeless people is the prevention of homelessness. Social workers are committed to understanding the causes of homelessness and providing appropriate support early on to prevent the loss of housing.

Social work with homeless people requires a holistic approach that addresses acute needs while aiming at long-term stabilization and social integration. By providing individually tailored services, social workers help improve the lives of homeless people and promote sustainable change.

Social work with the elderly

Social work with older people aims to promote the quality of life, well-being and social integration of older people.

Individual advice:

- Social workers provide individualized counseling for older people to help them cope with age-related challenges, losses, health issues, and other aspects of life.

Care Needs Assessment:

- Social workers conduct care needs assessments to identify older people's individual needs for support and care. This forms the basis for the development of care plans and the provision of services.

Promotion of self-employment:

- Social work aims to promote the independence of older people. This can include developing coping strategies, using assistive technologies, and adapting the environment.

Social integration:

- Social workers promote the social integration of older people, whether through participation in social activities, networking with community resources, or fostering social relationships.

Help to cope with losses:

- Losses, whether due to the death of loved ones, the loss of friends, or changes in health, can greatly affect older people. Social workers offer emotional support and help in coping with such losses.

Home care and support:

- Social workers assist older people in organising home care and support, whether through professional care services, volunteer support or the placement of nursing staff.

Financial Advice:

- The financial situation can be a challenge in old age. Social workers offer financial counseling to help older people manage their budget, apply for support, and other financial matters.

Activities for seniors:
- The organization of activities and programs for seniors helps to promote sociability, physical activity and mental stimulation. Social workers assist in identifying and participating in such activities.

Nursing home search and support:
- When moving to a nursing home becomes necessary, social workers assist older people and their families in selecting appropriate facilities, adapting to the new environment, and coping with change.

Mediation of support services:
- Social workers connect older people with various support services, whether in healthcare, home care, meal preparation, or other services that meet individual needs.

Social work with older people is based on a holistic approach that takes into account physical, social, emotional and financial aspects. Through targeted support, social workers help older people live dignified and fulfilling lives, regardless of the challenges of old age.

Social Worker Ethics

Ethics in social work plays a central role and forms the basis for professional conduct and the relationship between social workers and clients. The following are some basic principles and values of social work ethics:

Self-determination and autonomy:

- Social workers respect clients' right to self-determination and promote their autonomy. This means respecting clients' choices and goals and supporting them in choosing their own life paths.

Appreciation of uniqueness:

- Social workers treat each client as a unique individual with their own experiences, needs, values, and cultural backgrounds. The appreciation of diversity is a central principle of ethics.

Non-Discrimination and Justice:

- Social workers are committed to avoiding discrimination in any form and to advocating for social justice. They are actively working to reduce inequalities and promote equal opportunities.

Confidentiality and data protection:

- Social workers maintain the confidentiality of all information they receive in the course of their work. They respect the privacy of their clients and adhere to ethical and legal standards when handling sensitive data.

Professionalism and Integrity:

- Social workers act with integrity and ethical professionalism. This means acting honestly, transparently and responsibly, recognising one's own limits and behaving respectfully towards clients and other professionals.

Responsibility:

- Social workers take responsibility for their actions and decisions. They are aware of their role and strive to create positive change for their clients and society at large.

Continuous training:

- Ethics in social work requires a constant learning process. Social workers engage in continuous continuing education to update their skills and knowledge and ensure they are using effective and ethically sound practices.

Client-centered approach:

- The focus of social work is on the needs and desires of the clients. Social workers work together with their clients to set realistic goals and develop solutions together.

Respect for borders and dual relationships:

- Social workers are aware of the need to maintain clear boundaries and avoid dual relationships that could compromise the professional integrity and well-being of clients.

Reflection and Supervision:

- Social workers practice self-reflection and seek regular supervision to reconsider their actions and decisions and ensure that they are acting in an ethically responsible manner.

The professional ethics of social workers serves as a guide for professional conduct and helps to ensure the quality of social work. By adhering to ethical principles, social workers can build a trusting and respectful relationship with their clients and promote positive change in their lives.

Socialization

Socialization is the process by which individuals learn and internalize the norms, values, behaviors, and social skills of their society or community. This process usually takes place throughout life and affects how people see themselves, how they act in relationships, and how they function in their social environment.

Primary Socialization:

- Primary socialization takes place in the early years of life and is mainly carried out by the family and close caregivers. At this stage, children learn basic norms, values, and behaviors.

Secondary socialization:

- Secondary socialization occurs in later stages of life and involves other social institutions such as educational institutions, the workplace, and the media. Here, more specific skills and values are taught.

Agents of Socialization:

- Agents of socialization are individuals, groups, or institutions that influence the socialization process. This includes parents, siblings, teachers, peers, media, and religious institutions.

Role learning:

- Socialization involves learning social roles that are expected in a particular society or group. This includes gendered roles, job roles, and other social identities.

Norms and values:

- Norms are social rules that determine acceptable behavior in a society, while values are the basic beliefs and principles that are considered desirable. Both are internalized during socialization.

Identity Development:

- Socialization plays a crucial role in the development of personal identity. People learn who they are by confronting the expectations and values of their social environment.

Language:

- Socialization also influences the development of language. By interacting with others, individuals learn not only the language itself, but also the way it is used in different social contexts.

Social Skills Development:
- Socialization contributes to the development of social skills, which are crucial for successful interpersonal relationships. These include communication skills, empathy, and conflict resolution skills.

Cultural Socialization:
- Cultural socialization refers to the process by which people learn the cultural norms, traditions, and customs of their community. This includes cultural identity and cultural awareness.

Self-concept:
- Socialization influences the self-concept, i.e. the idea that individuals have of themselves. This includes aspects such as self-esteem, self-efficacy, and self-acceptance.

Socialization is a lifelong process that helps people function in their respective society or community. It not only shapes individual behavior, but also influences the structure and dynamics of societies.

Socio-pedagogical family assistance

Socio-pedagogical family assistance is an intensive, outreach form of youth welfare. Its aim is to support families in stressful life situations in order to strengthen the parenting skills of the parents and to positively influence the development of the children.

Outreach Assistance:
- The Socio-pedagogical family assistance is characterized by its outreach form. This means that the professionals go directly to the families' homes to offer support.

Individual support:
- The help is individually tailored to the needs of the family. The professionals work closely with the family members to work together to find solutions.

Family-centered work:
- The focus is on the family as a whole. The Socio-pedagogical family assistance does not only look at individuals, but also takes into account the dynamics and interactions within the family.

Strengthen parenting and everyday skills:
- One of the main goals of the Socio-pedagogical family assistance is to strengthen parents' parenting and everyday skills. This can include, for example, teaching parenting techniques, assistance in dealing with conflicts or support in organizing everyday family life.

Crisis intervention:
- The Socio-pedagogical family assistance also offers support in acute crisis situations. These can be, for example, conflicts in the family, difficulties at school or other acute problems.

Developmental support for children:
- Another goal is to positively influence the development of the children. This includes the promotion of academic achievement, social skills and a positive outlook on life.

Cooperation with other institutions:
- The Socio-pedagogical family assistance often works closely with other institutions and specialist services to create a comprehensive network for the families it serves. These include, for example, schools, offices, health facilities or therapeutic services.

Family involvement:
- Families are actively involved in the aid process. Their participation and co-determination are important principles in order to make aid as needs-oriented and acceptable as possible.

Long-term support:
- The support provided by the Socio-pedagogical family assistance is usually provided over a longer period of time. Through continuous support, a lasting change in the family's living situation is to be achieved.

Socio-pedagogical family assistance is an important form of educational aid, which is particularly characterized by its proximity to the living environment of the families and its holistic, resource-oriented way of working.

Sociotherapy

Sociotherapy is a form of therapeutic intervention that focuses on integrating social factors into the treatment process. In general, the term refers to therapeutic interventions in which social aspects and circumstances play an essential role.

Definition:
- Sociotherapy refers to therapeutic approaches that place social factors and relationships at the center of treatment. It aims to improve mental illness and social difficulties through interventions in a social context.

282

Holistic approach:

- Sociotherapy takes a holistic approach that not only looks at individual psychological symptoms, but also takes into account the social, family and cultural contexts in which a person lives.

Integration of social factors:

- Sociotherapeutic approaches integrate social factors such as family, friends, community, and professional circumstances into therapeutic planning. This may include identifying support systems, managing social stresses, and fostering positive social relationships.

Applications:

- Sociotherapy is used in various areas of psychiatry and psychotherapy, especially for people with severe mental illnesses affected by social difficulties.

Family Therapy:

- One subset of sociotherapy can be family therapy, where relationships within a family are considered as a key component of mental health.

Community-based approaches:

- Some sociotherapeutic interventions emphasize the strengthening of community resources and networks to promote social inclusion and well-being.

Outpatient care:

- Sociotherapy can be done on an outpatient basis and involves regular meetings with therapists or sociotherapists to work on the social factors that contribute to the maintenance or deterioration of mental health.

Collaboration with other professionals:

- In sociotherapy, therapists often work with other professionals, such as social workers, to provide comprehensive support for their clients' individual needs.

Long-term support:
- Sociotherapeutic interventions can provide long-term support because they aim to promote long-term changes in a person's social environment.

Preventive approach:
- Sociotherapy can also take a preventive approach to identify and manage social difficulties early on, before they lead to more serious mental health problems.

Sociotherapy emphasizes the interactions between individual mental health conditions and social factors. By integrating social aspects into therapy, this form of intervention can contribute to comprehensive and sustainable changes in the lives of those affected.

Speech therapy

Speech therapy is a therapeutic discipline that deals with the diagnosis, prevention, counseling, and treatment of speech, language, voice, and swallowing disorders. Speech therapists, also known as speech therapists, work with people of all ages, from children to adults, to improve their communication skills.

Diagnosis of speech and communication disorders:
- Speech therapists perform comprehensive diagnostic evaluations to identify speech, language, voice, and swallowing problems. This may include patient observation, interviews, and standardized testing.

Treatment of speech disorders:

- Speech therapy involves therapeutic interventions to treat speech disorders. This may include improving vocabulary, grammar, articulation, sentence structure, and other language skills.

Treatment of speech disorders:

- Speech therapists work with people who have difficulty speaking, whether due to slurred pronunciation, stuttering, or other speech disorders. Therapy may aim to improve speaking skills and increase intelligibility.

Treatment of voice disorders:

- Speech therapy may also include the treatment of voice disorders. This includes working on voice training, breath control, pitch, and other aspects to promote healthy and effective vocal communication.

Treatment of swallowing disorders:

- Speech therapists support people with swallowing disorders to ensure they can swallow food and fluids safely. This may include techniques to improve swallowing muscles and coordination.

Early intervention in children:

- Speech therapy plays an important role in early intervention in children with language delays or communication problems. Targeted interventions can mitigate possible developmental delays.

Advice and guidance:

- Speech therapists provide counseling and guidance to patients and their families. This may include tips on supportive communication at home, adapting the environment, and encouraging language development.

Collaboration with other professionals:

- Speech therapists often work in interdisciplinary teams with doctors, occupational therapists, teachers, and other professionals to provide comprehensive care for their patients.

Working with different age groups:

- Speech therapists work with people of all ages, from toddlers to seniors, depending on the specific needs and challenges of their patients.

Research and Continuing Education:

- Speech therapists are often involved in research and continuing education to keep their knowledge up to date and improve the quality of their services.

Speech therapy plays an important role in improving the quality of life of people with speech and communication disorders by helping them communicate more effectively and participate in social, school, and professional activities.

Subsidiarity

Subsidiarity is a principle that is applied in various contexts, including politics, ethics and the social sciences. The term is derived from the Latin word "subsidiarius", which means "helpful" or "supportive". The principle of subsidiarity generally states that tasks and responsibilities should be at the lowest possible level, unless there are compelling reasons to place them at a higher level.

Decentralization:

- Subsidiarity promotes the decentralisation of decisions and tasks. This means that preference should be given to local or smaller entities to sort things out, rather than it being done at a central or higher level.

Self-determination:
- The principle of subsidiarity emphasizes the self-determination and autonomy of individuals, groups or institutions. The point is that people should be able to manage their own affairs as much as possible.

Efficiency:
- Subsidiarity contributes to efficiency by ensuring that decisions are taken at the level where they can best be implemented. Local knowledge and resources can be used more effectively.

Responsibility:
- The principle of subsidiarity encourages the assumption of responsibility at local level. It encourages communities and institutions to take responsibility for their own affairs, rather than relying on centralized authorities.

Solidarity:
- Subsidiarity is linked to solidarity. Although tasks should be at lower levels, this does not mean that there cannot be collaboration between different levels. Solidarity can be built on a broader basis.

Protection of Freedom:
- The principle of subsidiarity protects individual freedom from excessive state interference. It emphasizes the idea that state authority should be limited and restrictive to ensure individual freedom.

Citizen participation:
- Subsidiarity promotes the participation of citizens in decision-making processes at local level. This strengthens democratic participation and gives people more influence over decisions that affect their community.

Legal certainty:
- The principle of subsidiarity helps to ensure legal certainty by defining clear competences and responsibilities. This

avoids confusion about who is responsible for certain tasks or problems.

Adaptability:

- Subsidiarity allows for better adaptation to local needs and circumstances. Local units can respond more flexibly to changes and take actions that are best suited to their specific circumstances.

Justice:

- The principle of subsidiarity contributes to the promotion of justice by ensuring that resources and opportunities are distributed fairly among local entities and that no one is unnecessarily patronised at the central level.

Subsidiarity is a fundamental principle that plays an important role in many political and social discussions. It emphasizes the importance of placing power and responsibility at the lowest possible level in order to promote individual freedom, self-determination, and efficiency.

Supervision

Supervision is a professional practice applied in various professional fields, including social work, health care, education, and psychology. It refers to a structured process in which an experienced supervisor accompanies and supports an individual or group of professionals to improve their professional development, skills, and performance.

Professional Development:
- Supervision aims to promote the professional development and growth of professionals. This can include the advancement of skills, knowledge, and personal effectiveness.

Reflection:
- A central aspect of supervision is reflection on professional practice. Professionals have the opportunity to reflect on their decisions, actions and reactions, while receiving supportive, critical and constructive feedback.

Quality assurance:
- Supervision serves quality assurance in professional contexts. By regularly reviewing and reflecting on working practices, standards can be maintained and improved.

Support in difficult situations:
- Professionals may encounter challenges and difficult situations in their work. Supervision provides a safe space to discuss these challenges, develop solution strategies, and receive emotional support.

Feedback and evaluation:
- Supervision involves providing constructive feedback on job performance. This may include identifying strengths, areas for development, and concrete actions to improve.

Self-reflection:
- Self-reflection is an essential part of supervision. Professionals are encouraged to reconsider their own values, attitudes and assumptions and to clarify their professional identity.

Confidentiality:
- Confidentiality is a fundamental principle of supervision. Professionals can talk openly about their challenges without this information being shared outside of the supervision context.

Relationship between supervisor and supervisor:
- The relationship between the supervisor and the person being supervised (supervisand) is of great importance. A supportive and trusting working alliance promotes effective supervision.

Multidisciplinary collaboration:
- Supervision can be used in different professional contexts and promotes multidisciplinary collaboration. Experts from different disciplines can learn from each other and work in a network.

Norms and Ethics:
- Supervision helps to maintain professional norms and ethical principles. This may include discussing ethical dilemmas, adhering to professional standards, and promoting ethical behavior.

Group supervision:
- In addition to individual supervision, there is also group supervision, in which several professionals are accompanied by a supervisor together. Group supervision enables the exchange of perspectives and experiences.

Further education:
- Supervision contributes to continuous professional development. By reflecting on current research, best practices, and new approaches, professionals can update their knowledge and skills.

Supervision is a dynamic and adaptable practice that helps to improve the quality of professional performance and support professionals to reach their full potential.

Supported employment

Supported employment is an approach to vocational rehabilitation aimed at facilitating access to the general labour market for people with disabilities. This approach focuses on the individual abilities, interests and needs of the individual and aims to provide supportive measures to enable successful integration into the labour market.

Target group:
- Supported employment is primarily aimed at people with different types of disabilities who have difficulties in finding and maintaining employment in the general labour market.

Individual planning:
- A central principle of supported employment is individual planning. Plans are made that take into account the abilities, interests and needs of the individual person.

Integration into the labour market:
- The main objective is to integrate people with disabilities into the general labour market, rather than employing them in specialised institutions or workshops.

Employer involvement:
- Employers play a crucial role in supported employment. The concept involves working with employers to create workplaces that meet the needs of people with disabilities.

Job coaching:
- Job coaching is an important part of supported employment. Job coaches support employees on site to ensure smooth integration and successful work performance.

Workplace adaptations:

- Workplace adjustments can be made as needed to ensure that the work environment meets the needs of employees with disabilities.

Flexibility:

- Supported employment is characterised by flexibility. The working hours, the type of work and the support measures are adapted to the individual requirements.

Inclusion and Diversity:

- The concept of supported employment promotes inclusion and diversity in the workplace. It helps to ensure that people with disabilities are recognised as equal members of the work environment.

Long-term support:

- Support doesn't end with hiring. Long-term support and follow-up are often part of the supported employment model to ensure sustainable integration into the labour market.

Measuring success:

- The success of supported employment is measured on the basis of long-term integration into the labour market and the achievement of individual goals.

Partnerships with service providers:

- Collaboration with various service providers, including vocational training institutions, rehabilitation facilities, and non-profit organizations, may be part of the supported employment model.

Legal basis:

- In many countries, there are legal regulations and programs that promote and support supported employment. These may include tax breaks, subsidies, or other incentives.

Supported employment is an important approach to promote the inclusion of people with disabilities in the labour market and helps them achieve their professional goals and reach their potential.

Sustainability

Sustainability refers to the ability to meet the needs of the present without jeopardizing the ability of future generations to meet their own needs. It is a multidimensional concept that encompasses environmental, social and economic aspects and aims to ensure balanced and long-term development.

Environmental sustainability:
- This aspect refers to the conservation and sustainable use of natural resources in order to protect the environment. This includes the responsible use of water, air, soil, biodiversity and the reduction of pollution.

Social Sustainability:
- Social sustainability focuses on ensuring social justice, equal opportunities, and a high quality of life for all people. This includes access to education, health care, social security, and the promotion of diversity and inclusion.

Economic sustainability:
- Economic sustainability aims to strike a balance between economic growth, efficiency, and securing resources for the future. This includes fostering innovation, fair trade, ethical business practices, and reducing dependence on non-renewable resources.

Efficiency:

- Sustainability requires an efficient use of resources to minimize waste. This includes measures such as recycling, renewable energy and the development of environmentally friendly technologies.

Circular economy:

- The idea of the circular economy refers to the concept that resources should be kept in closed loops rather than ending up as waste. This helps to minimize resource consumption and reduce waste.

Climate protection:

- Protection against the effects of climate change is a central component of sustainability. Measures to reduce greenhouse gas emissions, adapt to climate change and promote sustainable practices play a crucial role.

Participation and involvement:

- Sustainability requires the participation and co-determination of all relevant actors, including governments, businesses, civil society and individuals. The promotion of participation helps to create broad support for sustainable measures.

Global Cooperation:

- Since many sustainability issues are global in nature, international cooperation is crucial. This includes sharing knowledge, technologies, and resources to address common challenges.

Education for Sustainable Development:

- Education plays a crucial role in promoting sustainability. Education for sustainable development aims to give people an understanding of the complex interrelationships between the environment, society and the economy.

Temporal perspective:

- Sustainability requires a long-term perspective that takes into account the impact of decisions and actions on future generations. It's about finding a balance between the needs of the present and the future.

Sustainability is a fundamental concept for shaping a sustainable world that meets the needs of today's generation without compromising the opportunities of future generations. It is a holistic approach that integrates ecological, social and economic dimensions.

Systemic

The term "systemic" refers to an approach or perspective based on the principles of systems theory. Systems theory views phenomena as part of a larger whole, in which individual elements interact with each other and influence each other. The systemic perspective is applied in various disciplines such as psychology, psychotherapy, social work, organizational development, and others.

Holistic view:
- The systemic approach views problems and phenomena as part of a larger system. He attaches great importance to a holistic approach, in which not only individual parts are considered in isolation, but also the interactions between the parts and the overall system are taken into account.

Interaction and Relationship:
- Systems theory emphasizes the importance of interactions and relationships between the elements of a system. It is believed that changes in one part of the system can have an impact on the entire system.

Circularity instead of linearity:

- In systemic thinking, behavior or communication is often seen as circular rather than linear. This means that actions and reactions in a system are in constant interplay.

Self-organization and autonomy:

- Systems often have the capacity for self-organization and autonomy. This means that processes can occur within a system that are not centrally controlled, but arise from the interaction of the system elements.

Feedback Loops:

- Feedback loops are a central concept in systems theory. They represent the process by which effects of actions are returned to the system and taken into account in subsequent actions.

Ambiguity and Diversity:

- Systems can be ambiguous and diverse. This means that different perspectives and interpretations can exist, and that diversity in a system can be a resource.

Application in psychotherapy:

- In systemic psychotherapy, the systemic approach is applied to understand not only individual mental health problems, but also the dynamics and patterns in family, social, or organizational systems.

Organizational Application:

- In organizational development, the systemic approach is used to analyze the dynamics and interactions in organizations. Change is often not viewed in isolation at the individual level, but approached as part of organizational systems.

Family Therapy:

- Systemic approaches are often used in family therapy to understand family dynamics and interactions. The consideration of the entire family system is central to working with individual family members.

Social work:

- In social work, the systemic approach can be used to analyze the interactions between individual needs and social structures. The focus here is on the contextualization of individual challenges.

The systemic perspective emphasizes the interconnectedness, interaction, and complexity of systems, whether on an individual, family, organizational, or societal level. The approach is applied in various disciplines to provide a more comprehensive and contextualized view of problems and challenges.

Training-related assistance

The Training-Accompanying Assistance is a measure to support trainees during their vocational training. It is aimed in particular at adolescents and young adults who need support in the training process due to individual impairments or particular social difficulties. The training support includes the following key points:

Target group:

- The target group of the training-accompanying assistance are trainees who need special support due to individual impairments or social difficulties. These include, for example, young people with learning difficulties, a migrant background or social disadvantages.

Individual support:

- The training-related assistance offer individual support tailored to the needs and challenges of the individual trainee. This can include the promotion of professional, social or personal skills.

Learning support:

- A central aspect of the training assistance is the support for learning content at the vocational school and in the company. This may include tutoring, additional tuition, or other forms of learning support.

Socio-pedagogical support:

- In addition to professional support, the training-related assistance also offers socio-pedagogical support. This includes supporting the trainees in personal and social issues as well as promoting social skills.

Promotion of key skills:

- The training-related assistance promotes key qualifications that are important for the successful completion of training and entry into working life. These include, for example, communication skills, teamwork and self-organization.

Practical support during operation:

- In many cases, the assistance provided during training also includes practical support in the company. This can include adapting working conditions, teaching work techniques or helping them integrate into the business environment.

Consulting and Coaching:

- Training-related assistance offers counselling and coaching to support trainees in career planning, overcoming conflicts and other professional challenges.

Cooperation with training companies and vocational schools:

- The successful implementation of the training assistance requires close cooperation with the training companies and the vocational schools. This can include the coordination of teaching content, the organization of internships or integration into the company environment.

Integration into the labour market:

- The overarching objective of the training support is the successful integration of trainees into the labour market. This also includes support in finding a suitable job after completing the training.

Assistance during training helps to improve equal opportunities for trainees and to ensure their successful participation in the training process, especially when individual support is required.

Transculturality

Transculturality refers to the phenomenon of different cultures coming into contact with each other, interacting with each other, and influencing each other. It goes beyond the notion of culture as clearly delineated, homogeneous entities and acknowledges the diversity, dynamism and permeability of cultural boundaries.

Cultural exchange:

- Transculturality involves a lively cultural exchange between different groups and communities. This can be done through migration, trade, media, or other forms of interaction.

Hybridity:

- A central concept in transculturality is hybridity. This means that cultures are not rigid and immutable, but are constantly mixing, giving rise to new forms of expression and identities.

Cultural diversity:

- Transculturality emphasizes cultural diversity and the existence of multiple cultural influences within a community or a single person.

Intercultural Competence:

- In a transcultural environment, the development of intercultural competence is crucial. This includes the understanding and ability to interact effectively with people from different cultural backgrounds.

Cultural identity:

- Transculturality influences the construction of cultural identity. People can engage with different cultural influences in a transcultural environment and shape their own identity in a hybrid way.

Multiculturalism:

- Multiculturalism is closely linked to the idea of transculturality. It presupposes that different cultures can exist and be respected at the same time, without one being the dominant one.

Cultural Resilience:

- Transcultural situations often show cultural resilience, the ability of cultures and individuals to adapt to new contexts and preserve their identity despite cultural diversity.

Transnational Communities:

- Transculturality concerns not only the exchange within national borders, but also the transnational exchange of ideas, practices and identities.

Cultural Globalization:

- Transculturality is closely linked to cultural globalization, in which cultural products, ideas, and values are disseminated across national borders.

Cultural Conflicts and Harmony:
- In transcultural contexts, both cultural conflicts and cultural harmony can occur. It requires a sensitive understanding to foster positive interactions and manage conflict.

Cultural appropriation:
- A critical issue in transculturality is cultural appropriation, in which elements of one culture are adopted by another. It requires reflection on power relations and respect for cultural authenticity.

Cultural Sensitivity:
- Transculturality requires cultural sensitivity to avoid prejudice, value diversity, and recognize the need for inclusion and equity.

The concept of transculturality emphasizes the need for an open dialogue about cultural diversity and the influence of different cultures on individuals and societies. It promotes the appreciation of cultural diversity and the creation of inclusive, respectful and equitable communities.

Transitional allowance

Transition allowance refers to financial support paid in certain situations to help a person transition from one situation to another. This can include various contexts, including career transitions, rehabilitation, illness, or other life situations.

Rehabilitation:

- Transitional allowance is often paid in connection with rehabilitation measures, especially when someone is unable to carry out their regular job due to illness or injury.

Vocational rehabilitation:

- Persons who are no longer able to work in their previous profession due to health problems can receive a transitional allowance to support them during vocational rehabilitation or retraining.

Reintegration into the labour market:

- People who have been unemployed or are in a transition period to re-enter the labour market can receive transitional allowance to secure their livelihood during this period.

Unemployment:

- In some countries, transitional allowance can be paid as financial support during unemployment to facilitate the transition to new employment.

Sick pay:

- In the case of long-term illness, transitional allowance can be used as a form of sickness benefit to support the transition from incapacity for work due to illness to rehabilitation or return to work.

Requirements and duration:

- Eligibility for transitional allowance may vary by country and program. The duration of the payment often depends on the individual circumstances and the purpose of the payment.

Amount of payments:

- The amount of the transition allowance may depend on various factors, including the individual's income before the transition, the nature of the transitional measures, and the legislation of each country.

Integration of social benefits:

- In some cases, transition benefits can be combined with other social benefits, such as unemployment benefits or sick pay, to ensure a seamless transition.

Advice and support:

- Transition programs often also offer counseling and support to help the person plan and implement their transition.

Vocational rehabilitation:

- Transitional allowance can be used to help people reintegrate into the workforce after an illness or injury. This may also include the financing of retraining or other skills training.

Employer involvement:

- In some cases, transition allowance may also involve employer involvement, especially if the support is provided due to career changes or reorganisations.

Bridging allowance is intended to provide financial support to people in transition phases and to facilitate the transition to new living or working conditions. However, the exact conditions and regulations vary greatly depending on the country and context.

Trauma

Trauma refers to an extremely stressful or damaging experience that can have lasting emotional, psychological, or physical effects on a person. Traumatic experiences can take various forms, including physical violence, sexual abuse, natural disasters, accidents, war, neglect, loss of loved ones, and other life-threatening or drastic situations.

Types of trauma:
- Trauma can come in a variety of forms, including acute trauma (single events), chronic trauma (repeated or long-term exposure to stressful situations), and complex traumatization (combining different forms of trauma).

Psychological effects:
- Trauma can have a wide range of psychological effects, including post-traumatic stress disorder (PTSD), anxiety disorders, depression, dissociation, sleep disorders, and other mental health problems.

Physiological reactions:
- Trauma can also lead to physiological responses, such as increased stress, neurobiological changes in the brain, impaired hormonal balance, and other physical manifestations of stress.

Developmental trauma:
- Early childhood trauma or developmental trauma refers to stressful experiences in childhood that can interfere with normal development and emotional well-being.

Trauma management:
- People develop different coping mechanisms to deal with trauma. These include strategies such as avoidance, hypervigilance, dissociation or even healthy coping mechanisms such as social support, psychotherapy and self-care.

Post-traumatic stress disorder (PTSD):
- PTSD is a common mental health disorder that can occur after experiencing or confronting extremely stressful events. Symptoms include flashbacks, nightmares, increased irritability, and over-arousal.

Trauma-focused therapy:
- There are various therapeutic approaches that are specifically aimed at treating traumatic experiences. These include cognitive-behavioral therapy (CBT), EMDR (Eye Movement Desensitization and Reprocessing), trauma-focused cognitive behavioral therapy (TF-CBT), and others.

Cultural Sensitivity:
- Cultural sensitivity is important when it comes to treating trauma. Different cultures may have different ideas about trauma, and it's important to keep this in mind when supporting people.

Trauma-informed approaches:
- Trauma-informed approaches in various fields, including education, healthcare, and social work, take into account the impact of trauma and integrate practices that promote safety, stability, and empowerment.

Primary and secondary traumatization:
- Primary traumatization refers to the direct experience of traumatic events, while secondary traumatization can be the effects that result from supporting people who are traumatized themselves.

Resilience:
- Resilience refers to the ability to be resilient and recover after traumatic experiences. Resilient people can adapt and thrive despite difficult circumstances.

Societal impact:
- Trauma can have effects not only on individuals, but also on society. Societies can be affected by cultural traumas, such as historical injustices and collective trauma.

Working with traumatized people requires an empathetic understanding of the complex effects of trauma, as well as a supportive and respectful approach based on individual needs.

Trauma Pedagogy

Trauma pedagogy refers to a pedagogical approach that aims to understand and respond appropriately to the needs and challenges of people who have experienced trauma in educational contexts. The focus is on creating a safe and resource-oriented learning environment that takes into account the individual needs of those affected.

Awareness and understanding:
- Trauma pedagogy begins with raising awareness among educators and educational institutions about the effects of trauma. An understanding of the complexity of trauma and its potential impact on learning and behavior is critical.

Safety-Oriented Approach:
- A central tenet of trauma pedagogy is a safety-oriented approach. This means creating an environment that provides security and stability to give sufferers a sense of trust and well-being.

Resource orientation:
- Trauma pedagogy places a strong focus on resource orientation. The individual strengths and abilities of those affected are emphasized in order to promote their resilience.

Relationship building:
- The quality of the relationship between educators and learners plays a crucial role. Trauma pedagogy emphasizes the importance of safe and supportive relationships to build trust and foster emotional bonding.

Self-regulation skills:
- People who have experienced trauma may have difficulty self-regulating. Trauma pedagogy supports the development of self-regulation skills through targeted interventions and techniques.

Differentiated lesson design:
- Adapting teaching to different learning styles and needs is important in trauma pedagogy. This can mean catering to different speeds, learning modalities, and needs.

Empowerment:
- Empowerment is a central principle of trauma pedagogy. This includes empowering those affected so that they can take a more active role in their own learning process.

Trauma-sensitive classroom management:
- Class management in trauma pedagogical contexts takes into account the needs of traumatized learners. This can include strategies such as clear structures, predictable processes, and clear communication.

Trauma-informed methods:
- The use of trauma-informed methods and techniques is an essential part of trauma pedagogy. These may include mindfulness-based practices, artistic expressions, and other resource-oriented approaches.

Collective responsibility:
- Trauma pedagogy considers it important to promote a comprehensive understanding and collective responsibility for trauma-sensitive practices throughout the educational institution.

Training for educators:
- Educating educators in trauma-sensitive practices and trauma pedagogy is critical to ensuring high-quality support for traumatized learners.

Cooperation with experts:
- Working with trauma professionals, such as trauma therapists or social workers, can play an important role in trauma pedagogy to ensure comprehensive support.

Trauma pedagogy aims to make educational institutions safe and supportive places where traumatized learners can reach their full potential. Such an approach takes into account the diversity of experiences and supports the individual development of each learner.

Victim compensation

Victim compensation refers to financial and legal measures taken to support and compensate victims of crime or other harmful acts. The exact nature and extent of victim compensation may vary depending on a country's legal system and specific laws.

Financial compensation:
- Victims of crime may be entitled to financial compensation to cover the costs associated with the crime. These include medical expenses, therapy expenses, loss of income, property damage, and other financial burdens.

Rehabilitation support:
- Victims of serious crimes, especially those that result in physical or psychological injury, can receive rehabilitation support. This may include medical care, psychological care, and other forms of support.

Legal support:
- Victims may be entitled to legal assistance to represent their interests in criminal proceedings. This may include providing lawyers or assistance in applying for protection orders.

Victim protection:
- Victim compensation often includes measures to protect victims from further danger or harassment. This may

include, for example, protection orders against the offender or access to special protection programs.

Compensation fund:

- Many countries have special compensation funds or programs that provide financial assistance to victims of crime. These funds can be managed by government agencies or non-governmental organizations.

Recognition and support:

- Victim compensation often goes beyond financial aspects and includes the recognition and support of victims. This can be done through counseling services, help coping with trauma, and promoting social support.

Application and procedure:

- Many jurisdictions require victims to file a claim for victim compensation. Procedures and requirements may vary by country and legislation.

Victims' rights:

- Guaranteeing victims' rights, such as the right to information, participation in criminal proceedings and protection from harassment, is an important part of victim compensation.

Prevention of Victim Compensation:

- In addition to supporting victims, it is equally important to take preventive measures to prevent crime and harmful acts. This may include training, awareness campaigns, and enhanced safety measures.

Victim compensation is an important part of the justice system that aims to protect the rights and well-being of victims.

Vocational rehabilitation facilities

Vocational rehabilitation facilities are specialized facilities that help people with health impairments to improve their professional integration. These facilities offer various programs and services to meet the individual needs of participants. Some of the most common vocational rehabilitation facilities are:

Vocational Training Organisations (BFW):
- Vocational training centres are specialised institutions that offer comprehensive vocational rehabilitation programmes. They are designed to help people with health impairments develop or regain professional skills.

Vocational training centres (BBW):
- Vocational training centres are institutions that focus on the vocational training of people with disabilities. They offer practice-oriented training in various professional fields and support the integration of participants into the labour market.

Workshops for people with disabilities (WfbM):
- Workshops for disabled people are facilities where people with disabilities can work in protected working environments. Here, simple to complex jobs are often offered, and the aim is to promote professional skills and the ability to work.

Rehabilitation Centers:
- Rehabilitation centers often offer a wide range of services, including medical rehabilitation, vocational rehabilitation, psychosocial support, and therapeutic interventions.

Integration Services (IFD):
- Integration services are service providers that support people with disabilities in their integration into the general

labour market. They offer individual advice, placement and support in the workplace.

Service providers of vocational rehabilitation:

- Service providers, such as the Employment Agency or the Pension Insurance, play a decisive role in the financing and organisation of vocational rehabilitation measures.

Funding and Integration Offices:

- Funding and Integration Offices are regional authorities that are responsible for the implementation of vocational rehabilitation measures. They support people with disabilities in participating in working life.

Social Psychiatric Services:

- For people with mental illnesses, social psychiatric services can provide support for vocational rehabilitation. This can include advice, guidance and support in finding suitable jobs.

Counselling centres for rehabilitation:

- There are specialised counselling centres that provide people with disabilities and their relatives with information and advice on the possibilities of vocational rehabilitation.

Inclusive businesses:

- Inclusive companies are workplaces that are designed to integrate people with disabilities into the regular labour market. Here, people with and without disabilities work together.

These vocational rehabilitation facilities play a crucial role in helping people with health impairments achieve their professional goals and successfully integrate into the labour market. The type of support varies depending on the individual needs of the participants and the respective health challenges.

Vocational Training Centre

A vocational training centre is an institution that focuses on vocational training and qualification of young people with special needs. The target group is usually adolescents and young adults with health impairments, learning difficulties or other individual difficulties that make it difficult to access the regular education system.

Target group:
- Vocational training centres are aimed at young people who have difficulties in making the transition from school to work due to health impairments or other individual challenges.

Vocational education and training:
- The main goal of a vocational training centre is vocational education and training. The institutions offer a wide range of training occupations to suit the individual interests and abilities of the participants.

Individual support:
- Each participant is supported individually, with special attention paid to individual needs, abilities and learning styles. This may also include specialized educational and therapeutic support.

Practical training:
- Training at a vocational training centre often includes intensive practical training. Participants will have the opportunity to develop and test their skills in real work environments.

Socio-pedagogical support:
- In addition to technical training, vocational training centres offer socio-educational support. This can include support with personal challenges, social skills and the development of independence.

Teaching of working techniques:
- Participants not only learn technical skills, but are also trained in working techniques, work organisation and other key competences that are important for successful integration into the labour market.

Transition from school to work:
- Vocational training centres play a crucial role in the transition from school-based education to working life. They offer support in choosing a career and prepare participants to act independently in their careers.

Cooperation with companies:
- Many vocational training centres cooperate with companies in order to arrange internships and apprenticeships for the participants. This promotes integration into the regular labour market.

Aftercare:
- After completion of the training, some vocational training centres offer follow-up services to support the former participants in their professional integration and to accompany them in their further careers.

Advice and support:
- Vocational training centres also offer advice and support on personal, social and professional issues in order to create the best possible conditions for the development of participants.

Vocational training centres are institutions that help to improve the career prospects of young people with special needs and to promote their participation in working life.

War Victims' Care

War victims' welfare refers to measures and services for people who have been physically or psychologically harmed by wars, armed conflicts or other violent conflicts. This support can take different forms and is regulated differently depending on the country and legal system.

Health care:
- War victims may require specialized medical care, including rehabilitation, physical therapy, psychological care, and long-term medical treatment.

Financial support:
- Many countries have systems of financial assistance to war victims, which may include pensions, compensation, or other cash benefits. This financial support is intended to cover the cost of living and to provide some financial security to those affected.

Rehabilitation and reintegration:
- War victim care may include rehabilitation and social reintegration programmes. This may include vocational training, workplace support, and other initiatives to promote self-employment.

Legal aspects:
- There are special laws and regulations to protect and support war victims. These laws can regulate compensation claims and ensure that the rights of those affected are respected.

Assistance for the disabled:
- People who have been disabled by acts of war can receive special assistance in the field of disability assistance. This may include the provision of tools, barrier-free access to

public facilities and other measures to promote participation.

Psycho-social support:

- Due to the often traumatic experiences associated with wars, psycho-social support programs may be necessary. Psychological care and support in coping with trauma are important components of war victim care.

International support:

- In some cases, international organizations such as the International Committee of the Red Cross (ICRC) or the United Nations (UN) can play a role in supporting war victims by providing humanitarian assistance and supporting reconstruction and rehabilitation programs.

Compensation:

- Victims of war may be entitled to compensation, especially if their injuries are the result of war crimes or acts contrary to international law.

Social integration:

- An important aspect of war victim care is the promotion of social integration and acceptance of people affected by conflicts. This may include public awareness, training programs, and other measures to overcome bias.

The care of war victims is a complex issue that encompasses various areas of support. The exact design depends on the specific circumstances, the country in question and the international regulations. It is important that those affected have access to the services they need to regain their quality of life and achieve a certain normality in their lives.

Welfare

Social assistance is a form of government assistance provided to people in financial distress in order to secure their livelihood and enable them to participate in social life.

Objective of social assistance:
- The main goal of social assistance is to help needy people in financial distress and to enable them to secure their livelihood and participate in social life.

Authorized persons:
- As a rule, persons who are unable to support themselves from their own resources due to unemployment, illness, disability, old age or other special circumstances are entitled to social assistance.

Livelihood:
- Social assistance ensures a secure livelihood through financial support in the form of cash benefits. These benefits are intended to cover the cost of food, clothing, shelter, health care, and other basic needs.

Needs assessment:
- The amount of social assistance benefits is based on an individual needs assessment procedure. The personal and financial circumstances of the applicant will be taken into account.

Types of social assistance:
- Social assistance can take various forms, including subsistence assistance, basic support for old age and reduced earning capacity, health assistance, integration assistance for people with disabilities and care assistance.

Application Process:
- In order to receive social assistance, applicants must submit an application to the relevant social welfare office. In this

application, they must disclose their personal and financial circumstances.

Principle of subordination:

- Social assistance follows the principle of subordination, which means that benefits are only granted when all other possible means of assistance and support have been exhausted, including the use of one's own assets.

Income and asset imputation:

- When calculating social assistance, the applicant's income and assets are taken into account. There are allowances, and certain income or assets are not taken into account.

Social Assistance and Labour Integration:

- In some countries, there are programmes for the labour integration of welfare recipients. These aim to promote integration into the labour market and reduce dependence on government support.

Legal context:

- Social assistance arrangements may vary from country to country or region. The legal framework and precise conditions are determined by national or regional laws and regulations.

Social assistance plays an important role in the social security system by supporting people in need and enabling them to live in dignity.

Work Assistance

Work assistance refers to support services that people with disabilities receive in the workplace in order to promote their integration into the labour market and enable their participation in the labour market. This support can be provided both during the application process and during the employment itself.

Professional integration:
- Work assistance aims to facilitate access to the labour market for people with disabilities. This includes support in the job search, application and hiring process.

Individual needs analysis:
- Work assistants often conduct an individual needs assessment to identify the specific support needs of a person with disabilities. This may include physical, sensory, cognitive, or psychosocial aspects.

Workplace adaptations:
- Assistance in adapting the workplace to take into account the individual abilities and needs of the worker with disabilities. This may include the provision of special work equipment, adjustments to working hours or ergonomic changes.

Training and Coaching:
- Training and coaching can be provided to strengthen the skills and independence of the employee with disabilities. This can include both technical and social skills.

Support in everyday work:
- Helping them cope with day-to-day challenges in the workplace, whether through personal assistance, communication support, or any other assistance needed.

Promoting accessibility:
- Work assistance also aims to break down barriers in the workplace and create a barrier-free environment. This can include physical accessibility, but also accessibility of information and communication.

Promoting self-determination:

- An important aspect of work assistance is to promote the self-determination and autonomy of people with disabilities. This means that they are actively involved in decisions regarding their professional participation.

Cooperation with employers:

- Work assistants work closely with employers to ensure that the needs and abilities of people with disabilities are optimally addressed. This may include raising awareness of inclusion and diversity in the workplace.

Work assistance is essential for the equal participation of people with disabilities in working life. It promotes equal opportunities and helps to ensure that individual skills and potential can be used in the best possible way.

Work integration

Labour integration refers to the process of successfully integrating people into the labour market, especially those who have difficulties finding or keeping a job due to various barriers. This integrative approach aims to promote individual skills, overcome barriers and enable sustainable professional participation.

Individual needs analysis:

- A thorough analysis of each individual's skills, qualifications, and needs is crucial. This makes it possible to offer targeted support and training.

Career Guidance and Counselling:

- Support in the identification of professional goals, interests and strengths. Career counseling helps to set realistic and achievable career goals.

Qualification measures:

- Providing training, education or skills to improve the skills and knowledge of jobseekers and increase their employability.

Placement in work:

- Assist with the job search and application process, including the preparation of resumes and cover letters. Work integration services can also help in contacting potential employers.

Workplace adaptations and workplace support:

- If necessary, adjustments are made in the workplace to accommodate individual needs. Workplace support can also include training for employers and colleagues to promote an inclusive work environment.

Social integration:

- Work integration includes not only occupational but also social integration. This can include fostering teamwork, communication skills, and creating a supportive work environment.

Long-term support:

- Support doesn't end with hiring. Long-term mentoring and follow-up are often necessary to ensure that the integration is stable and sustainable.

Cooperation with employers and companies:

- Working closely with employers is crucial to breaking down barriers, overcoming biases and creating an inclusive work environment.

Integration into the labour market is relevant, especially for groups that may be disadvantaged in the labour market, such as people with disabilities, the long-term unemployed or migrants. An inclusive approach not only contributes to the quality of life of individuals, but also to the creation of a more inclusive and diverse world of work.

Workshop for Disabled People

The Workshop for Disabled People is an institution that provides people with disabilities with a sheltered workplace to develop their professional skills, train them and pursue meaningful employment. These workshops are part of vocational rehabilitation and are intended to give people with disabilities the opportunity to develop their individual potential and strengthen their professional skills.

Sheltered workplace:
- The Workshop for Disabled People offers a sheltered workplace for people with different types of disabilities. This allows for a customized environment that is tailored to the needs of employees.

Vocational education and training:
- Within the Workshop for Disabled People, participants receive vocational training and qualification in various fields of work. This can include both craft and industrial activities.

Individual support:
- The programs in the workshop are designed to promote the individual skills and potential of the participants. This often involves the creation of individual support plans.

Areas of work and projects:
- In Workshop for Disabled People, different areas of work can exist, depending on the skills and interests of the

participants. This includes manual work, assembly and packaging tasks, horticulture, housekeeping and more.

Work instructions and supervision:

- Participants will receive guidance and supervision from professionals to ensure that work tasks match individual skills and needs.

Participation in working life:

- The workshop enables people with disabilities to participate in working life and helps to strengthen their independence and self-esteem.

Wage:

- In some countries, Workshop for Disabled People participants receive a salary. This can be based on the individual performance or a lump sum. In other cases, the focus is on rehabilitation and vocational training, and no regular salary is paid.

Preparation for the general labour market:

- Some Workshop for Disabled People programmes aim to prepare participants for possible integration into the general labour market. This can be done through internships, career orientation or special support programmes.

Social integration:

- Participants will also have the opportunity for social integration and participation in community activities within the workshop and beyond.

The design and design of workshops for disabled people can vary depending on where they are staying, as this depends on the respective legal and social conditions. In many cases, however, the promotion of self-determination, participation and professional skills is at the heart of the programmes.

Youth welfare office

The Youth Welfare Office is an institution at the municipal level that deals with issues relating to the well-being of children and young people. It plays a central role in child and youth welfare law and takes on various tasks in the context of protecting, promoting and supporting young people.

Child protection:
- One of the main concerns of the Youth Welfare Office is the protection of children from neglect, abuse, exploitation and other forms of endangerment. It intervenes when a child's well-being is at risk.

Educational aids:
- The Youth Welfare Office offers various educational aids to support parents and families in difficult life situations. This includes counselling, care, family support, educational assistance and therapeutic measures.

Youth Welfare Planning:
- The Youth Welfare Office is responsible for the planning and organisation of youth welfare measures at the local level. This includes the identification of needs, the coordination of offers and cooperation with other relevant institutions.

Adoption Brokerage:
- In many countries, the Youth Welfare Office plays a role in arranging adoptions. It assesses the suitability of adoptive parents, supports adoption processes and ensures the well-being of the adopted child.

Youth work:
- The Youth Welfare Office promotes youth work and youth protection measures. It supports youth centres, projects,

leisure activities and educational opportunities for young people.

Child and Adolescent Psychiatry:

- In some cases, the Youth Welfare Office may be involved in arranging child and adolescent psychiatry, especially if mental health problems affect a child's well-being.

School Social Work:

- Cooperation with schools and school social workers is one of the tasks of the Youth Welfare Office. This may include support from students, parents, and teachers.

Day care:

- The Youth Welfare Office is also responsible for the planning and supervision of childcare facilities, such as kindergartens and crèches.

Assistance for upbringing in case of endangerment of the child's well-being:

- If the well-being of a child is acutely endangered, the Youth Welfare Office can take necessary protective measures, including taking the child into care.

Advice and information:

- The Youth Welfare Office offers advice and education on various topics in the field of child and youth welfare in order to support and inform families.

The exact responsibilities and tasks may vary in the regional context, but in general the Youth Welfare Office is responsible for ensuring the well-being of children and young people and promoting their positive development.

Thank you for your interest in this book

The satisfaction of our readers is important to us, and we would be very happy if you could send us your feedback on the book.

We would like to ask you to take a moment to write a customer review on Amazon. In this way, you support other readers in making purchasing decisions and contribute to the continuous improvement of our offering.